D1366066

MOUNTAIN FLOWERS

MOUNTAIN FLOWERS

Adapted from the text of
UBERTO TOSCO

With a foreword by Christopher Humphries PhD, BSc, ALS
Curator of the European Herbarium, British Museum (Natural History)

ORBIS PUBLISHING · London

Contents

Frontispiece: Tree groundsels, with Mount Kenya in the background (Alan Wearing/Ardea) Endpapers: Prickly saxifrage (J. & D. Bartlett/Bruce Coleman)

© Istituto Geografico de Agostini, Novara 1973
English edition © Orbis Publishing Limited, London 1974
This edition published in 1978
Originally published as The World of Mountain Flowers
Adapted from the original Italian, *flora alpina*
Printed in Italy by IGDA, Novara
ISBN 0 85613 004 4

Foreword

In our time, the writing and publication of natural history books is an important service to all mankind. There has been no other period in history with so many man-made resources avaiable for the observation and study of the plants and animals living around us. By the same token, however, there has been no other period when man has had such an irreversibly drastic effect on all other organisms inhabiting the earth, with the consequence that increasing numbers are being lost forever. There are more people alive today than have ever lived before, and, if mankind intends to survive, to do so he must learn to live in a delicate and harmonious balance with other forms of life, in a unified ecological system.

For these reasons, the publication of this book is a timely event. Mountain flowers and their environments are among the most beautiful and spectacular elements of the world's natural treasures, and the first-rate photographs of the vivid flower colours and breath-taking alpine scenery can only serve to enhance the reader's appreciation of nature.

The vegetation found on mountains throughout the world is composed of such a bewildering variety of beautiful herbs, grasses, shrubs and trees that few people can be expected to have a knowledge of more than a fraction of them. To overcome this difficulty, the author of this book has taken a satisfying approach by comparing predominant vegetation cover and principal plant species in some of the most spectacular mountains of the world.

Mountains are meeting places for many floristic elements, each related to the variable rainfall, topography, altitude, and the various soils and rocks. We find many distinct vegetation zones which are often closely associated with one another; examples include the broadleaved deciduous woods, the conifer forests, the grasslands, the tundra and the alpine scrub. These communities, together with the mountain environment, give us many indigenous flowering plants of exceptional colour, form and beauty – species quite unlike any which grow elsewhere.

So rich are the mountain floras that no book of this kind can possibly illustrate more than a fraction of them. So as to indicate the splendour of the most characteristic plants and vegetation which we might find in the mountains, the author and photographers have concentrated much of their effort on the European Alps. In this way they are not only able to demonstrate the beauty of many a small and 'ordinary' flower which the majority of people pass over unnoticed, but have also had the opportunity to explain something about the botanical history of high mountains, the principal adaptations, the climatic variations, the floristic elements and even the medical uses of mountain flowers.

CHRISTOPHER HUMPHRIES

Index

Page references to photographs are printed in *italics*.

Latin names

Note on the use of capital initials

The term 'Alpine' with a capital initial is used in this book to mean 'of the European Alps' in a geographical sense; 'alpine', without a capital initial, is used to mean 'montane' in the general sense.

Capital initials have also been used for common names which denote individual species so that they can be more readily recognized.

Alpine landscapes and flowers

Mountain landscape along the road through the Sella Pass in the Dolomites. In the foreground tufts of a willowherb (species of Epilobium) *are growing at the side of a brook. Beyond the conifer wood the characteristically and dramatically jagged peaks of the Dolomites*

The broad plains of the earth, often stretching vast distances beyond the horizon, show woods, grasslands and fields of crops, which, while harbouring hundreds of plant species, still maintain a certain degree of floristic homogeneity. The pattern thus presented tends to vary, however, according to both latitude and altitude, and these determining physical factors, together with the climate which is related to them, imprint an almost uniform character upon the vegetation. For instance, in the Arctic tundras there are to be found mosses, lichens, grasses, flowers and stunted bushes, identical or very similar to those growing in the high mountains. This almost gives the impression that the tundra is simply an extensive complex of the alpine slopes ironed out into a single, vast plain. In the same way, therefore, that one moves from the temperate through to the sub-Arctic and Arctic zones, the climb from the lowlands along the valleys and up the alpine slopes brings into view a similar vegetation type which often contains the same plants.

The alpine flora, however, is not identical in all mountainous areas. A mountain chain or massif very frequently contains its own characteristic species, and these are sometimes what naturalists term 'endemics', plants which are very strictly confined to specific localities.

1

After the glaciations which have affected vast areas of the earth in past ages and have formed many of the major geographical features in alpine areas, certain species were able to survive, preserved for thousands of years in zones which remained intact between the glaciers. Nowadays, we define these plants as 'glacial relicts'.

Naturally, in those areas of the earth which escaped glaciation, such as the tropics, the mountain ranges have preserved a different type of vegetation. In the tropics altitude and climatic conditions have allowed a succession of belts to develop, each having a different floristic structure.

All of those considerations which act in different ways to create the complexity of the alpine flora will be considered in this book one by one.

Although it is probable that no two mountain areas contain the same plant species, they do

(Above) The meadows of this valley merge with the conifer woods which rise as far as the pastures and the alpine tundra. The foliage of the larch in the foreground is golden, which shows that it is autumn

(Right) Flowers in full bloom in the Glacier National Park, Montana

develop distinct, recognizable vegetation patterns such as the alpine tundra, the coniferous forests and montane grasslands, to mention just three. We can now briefly outline the principal mountain areas which develop characteristic floras.

For the purposes of this book we can divide the world into four main regions: the Old World (which includes Europe, Africa and the Middle East), the New World (which includes the Americas), Asia and Australasia.

The principal mountains of the Old World

include the European Alps, the Pyrenees and Appennines, the equatorial mountains of Africa in Uganda, Tanzania, Ethiopia, the Camerouns and the central slopes of Madagascar. The predominant New World mountains can include the Appalachians, the Rockies and the highlands of Mexico in North America and the Andean cordilleras of Colombia, Peru, Bolivia and Argentina in South America. The most important Asian mountain chain is undoubtedly the Himalayas but the highlands of Java, Sumatra and Borneo are also interesting.

While considering the technicalities and the intricacies of mountain flowers, however, it is best always to retain our sense of perspective and to remember that we are discussing nature at her most grand and at her most exquisite. The mountains of the world present awesome prospects yet little can compare with the delight of discovering for oneself the miniature beauty of a rare species. The variety and intensity of colour, the multitude of shapes and structures among the mountain flowers are a constant source of wonder to those who study them.

(Above) Ampola Lake in the Trentine Alps; the surface of the lake is, for the most part, covered with water-lily leaves and flowers

(Left) Astragalus centroalpinus *var.* alopecuroides, *a rare leguminous plant found in some parts of the Aosta Valley*

4

Alpine vegetation and flora

Larchwood in the Aosta Valley, one of the most common and characteristic types of conifer woods. A wood like this one can present certain habitat variations which allow differences in the floristic composition of the ground flora

The words vegetation and flora are often confused by those unacquainted with them, yet they have very different meanings. In fact, the former refers to the whole assemblage of plants which covers a zone or a locality in a more or less compact, often homogenous community. The latter, flora, must be taken as a kind of simple list of diverse plant species which make up the green and flowered carpet.

And so it is natural to speak of both the alpine flora and of the alpine vegetation, but in the first case it is sufficient to distinguish, identify and present the hundreds of species which grow on a mountain or a mountain range, on the under-

standing that each species is equal to any other in value. So, we have the rarest rock plants such as the Dwarf alpine forget-me-not *(Myosotis alpina)*, the Alpine toadflax *(Linaria alpina)*, and the Edelweiss *(Leontopodium alpinum)* growing side by side with the widespread, humble Mat-grass *(Nardus stricta)* and the very common mosses.

When, instead, we want to illustrate the vegetation of a mountain, we must understand what botanists call the plant community and study its limits, composition, and vitality. Thus we can distinguish communities such as forest groups (like beechwoods, and larchwoods), shrub

Alpine pastureland at an altitude of about 2,300 m in the Piedmont. The vegetation consists mainly of grasses and sedges; in particular the sedge Carex sempervirens

lands (like those of rhododendrons) and, finally, grasslands like the luxuriant grasslands in the valleys of the European Alps or the various types of alpine-like steppe or tundra. These grasslands are distinguished by the predominant species within the community; for instance, Mat-grass (dominated by the grass *Nardus stricta*), evergreen steppe (dominated by *Carex sempervirens*), fescue sward (dominated by grass species of the genus *Festuca*), and the curved sedge steppe (after the dominant species *Carex curvula*).

Naturally, the concepts of flora and vegetation are closely allied to each other inasmuch as the flora is primarily a systematic, more or less rational cataloguing of the species which constitute a vegetation type, just as a particular vegetation type is absolutely characterized by its floristic components. As examples, siliceous rocks situated at a certain altitude will have a floristic composition that characterizes the type of vegetation; an expanse of mountain forest of more or less homogeneous composition will consist, in a similar way, of thousands of plants which

will often belong to only a very limited number of species.

It is interesting to note that by studying the vegetation of a specific zone it is possible to determine the percentages of the species which are present. Thanks to the possibility of attributing each species to a particular geographical, climatic and ecological element, it is obvious that each type of vegetative community under examination can be ascribed a set of environmental characteristics dictated by its origins (which may be very remote), by the climate, and by the conditions in which the community exists.

Thus, in studying an area like the European Alps, for example, students of geobotany will distinguish a steppe-type wood with elements predominantly of Asiatic origin, moorland with species mainly of Atlantic origin, xerothermic relict vegetation of European origin, and so forth.

The various types of soil will obviously assist different vegetations; perhaps the most characteristic example is the Dolomitic flora on calcareous rock. Wet, acid conditions produce bogs and marshes with their accompanying vegetation.

Aspect, too, plays an important role due to the differences in temperature and rainfall. A beechwood, for instance, will look very different on northern and southern slopes.

Origins of alpine flora

As with any other group of living organisms, selected systematically, ecologically or geographically, we must now consider how the great variety of extant alpine plants have been produced as the result of complex, remote and slow physico-climatic transformations which have affected the various mountain systems of the earth and the territories around them.

Naturally these considerations, are valid for all massifs and mountain chains though each range may have undergone a different rate of change. It is thus sufficient here to limit examples above all to the Alps and the other European mountains which were formed about the beginning of the Tertiary Period when Europe was largely covered with thick, luxuriant vegetation (mostly forest), in a subtropical climate.

As the colossi of rock took shape in all their majesty and grandeur, a number of the plants from the lowlands gradually adapted and occupied territories at higher altitudes, the adaptations coming about through various evolutionary phenomena. Naturally, a few particular plant families have given the Alpine flora its greatest number of species and these families are responsible not only for European montane species but also for many non-European ones.

Consequently, we can list the most commonly represented flowering plant families as the *Gentianaceae*, the *Ranunculaceae*, the *Cruciferae* or *Brassicaceae*, the *Saxifragaceae*, the *Caryophyllaceae*, the *Compositae*, the *Ericaceae*, the *Crassulaceae*, the *Primulaceae*, the *Campanulaceae* and the *Gramineae*.

Some time after this formation of the Alpine floristic structure, during the Quaternary Period, there were gradual modifications in the climate which are still not thoroughly understood and which affected the Northern Hemisphere in particular to bring about a spreading of glaciation from the poles culminating in an ice age.

The result was the formation of a great system of glaciers which covered all the regions of Arctic and sub-Arctic Eurasia, eliminating almost all terrestrial continuity. At the same time, powerful glaciers formed in the Alpine valleys, not only on the northern slopes but also on the southern ones, invading parts of the Po Valley, the Rhône Valley and so on.

The advance and the expansion of the glaciers forced the plants of the Arctic and Alpine regions which had established themselves in new localities to retreat. In this way the Arctic, sub-Arctic and Alpine 'elements' of the flora came into contact in a territory bounded by the ice shield to the north and the Alpine cap to the south, where eventually this 'Arctic-Alpine' flora took a hold.

As is well known, there were four main ice ages (the Gunz, the Mindel, the Riss and the Würm), the first three of which were most distinct and

(Right) One of the most interesting endemics among the Alpine flora is Campanula thyrsoides *which grows at altitudes between 1,500 m and 2,700 m, preferring rich pastureland on calcareous soils*

separated by more or less long interglacial periods during which the temperature rose and the climate became milder.

The increase in temperatures brought about a gradual recession of the glaciers which was followed – if one can put it that way – by an advance of the flora up the Alpine valleys, often reaching the exposed peaks from their point of departure, the meeting place of the original Arctic and Alpine floras. During this re-occupation of terrain which had been lost to the glaciers, many species became extinct or at least survived only in a very limited sense, while others advanced to a greater or lesser extent so that in the end there was a highly heterogeneous distribution; a factor also controlled to some extent by the variable degrees of adaptability of the plants.

Many other plants, on the other hand, remained isolated on the peaks and rocks which had newly emerged from the retreating glaciers, and their increased distribution became possible only after a more complete withdrawal of the glaciers. These 'islands' of refuge are usually called 'nunnataks'.

There were also many species of the Arctic-Alpine flora which, by adapting to the new pioneer settlement areas, climbed the valleys and the slopes until they reached the peaks or the plateaux, accessible between one glaciation and another, which provided new sites eminently suitable for alpine plants. In other cases a few species, as they advanced, settled in zones which were not typically alpine but which, having a cold climate, offered them a suitable habitat often limited and typified by special physical peculiarities, such as cold ravines and peat-bogs.

So it was that on the return to a mild climate, many species which had gradually adapted to the new conditions, remained and survived in localities not only non-alpine in character, but also far from the peaks which had harboured them. A good example of this phenomenon is *Pinguicula alpina* which even within living memory, grew in a cold ravine on a hill several kilometres from Turin beyond the River Po, some distance from the Alpine range.

Botanists – as we have already said – distinguish these plants now marooned in the places which they occupied during the periods of glaciation and interglaciation as glacial relicts. Many alpine endemics or, in other words, those plant species distributed in small, isolated areas originated in this way.

Alpine endemics include some species of the *Saxifragaceae (Saxifraga biflora, S. seguieri, S. muscoides)* two *Compositae (Achillea moschata,* and the dwarf species *A. nana)*, the Yellow house-leek *(Sempervivum wulfenii)* and a lovely, rare campanula with yellow flowers which grow in compact spikes, *Campanula thyrsoides*. There are plenty of Alpine flowers with an even narrower distribution, such as the Engadine gentian, *(Gentiana engadinensis)* of the Engadine Valley, the Valley primrose *(Primula daonensis)*, limited, as the name suggests, strictly to the Daone Valley in the central Alps, and *Aquilegia einseleana* which is limited to the central-eastern Alps.

(Above) Alpine landscape in Lombardy during mid-summer. The pastures on the rocky slopes are dotted with flowering bushes of rhododendrons and the sulphur-yellow flowers of the Spotted gentian (Gentiana punctata)

(Far left) Glacier buttercup or crowfoot (Ranunculus glacialis).
(Left) Mountain avens (Dryas octopetala); both these species are characteristic of Artic-Alpine flora

Of the plants which indicate by their present distribution their distribution in past ages, i.e. those in Arctic territories and the Alps (Arctic-Alpine species), we should also mention the white or pink Glacier buttercup *(Ranunculus glacialis)*, the Livelong saxifrage *(Saxifraga paniculata)*, which occurs on exposed rocks, *Saxifraga aizoides* with its red-speckled yellow flowers, which abounds along meadow brooks and in Alpine peat-bogs, as well as the Mountain avens *(Dryas octopetala)* and the delicate Twin-flower *(Linnaea borealis)*.

Other species are placed among the so-called 'Altaico-Alpine' element and are to be found on the Alps and in the mountains of northern Asia. This group includes the Edelweiss *(Gnaphalium leontopodium* or *Leontopodium alpinum)* which also has sister species on other mountain chains including the distant Himalayas.

Also worth a mention are two other groups of plants which we can find in the Alpine flora: those growing in caves in almost complete darkness and those that prefer grassy, sunny slopes.

In the first category, we can quote the classical example of the so-called Luminescent moss *(Schistastega osmundacea)*. These tiny plants are only a few millimetres high and form a carpet on the damp walls of siliceous, rocky caves. The young thalli (or protonemes) possess a layer of cells capable of refracting whatever light may strike them. Consequently, the clumps of moss stand out with an emerald-green glitter.

It is currently thought that this and other mosses now found in the caves once lived outside them, under cover in areas where there was a lot of damp, or in cold, shady ravines. It was the higher temperatures of the interglacial and post-glacial periods which forced them into the shelter of the caves where they are still found today.

The second group of plants, containing those which need the light and the heat of the sun, as we will explain later, immigrated to the Alps, the Apennines and the Pyrenees of Europe from the warm steppes of Asia. Just one example from this group is the elegant and much sought after Feather grass *(Stipa pennata)*.

9

Characteristics and adaptations

Few living organisms can suddenly adapt to an environment totally different from the one in which they originated and to which their progenitors had been conditioned by nature over great periods. Only man can, in a few days (or nowadays in a few hours thanks to modern transport) travel from the equator to the poles without succumbing to the vastly different climatic and environmental conditions.

But man, obviously, is endowed not only with a capacity for adaptation, but also with the possibility of resisting sudden changes of environment and keeping himself in tolerable conditions by means of a host of survival stratagems.

Most other animals and plants, however, can adapt or acclimatize only very slowly to new conditions; and not every species is capable of adapting at all. Many alpine plants, as we said in the previous chapter, did not originate in montane localities but gradually migrated to higher altitudes from the surrounding lowlands. The Arctic-Alpine and the alpine elements were generally unable to adapt to the changing lowland climate and so became isolated in only a few suitable montane habitats.

Some common characteristics peculiar to hypsophilic plants (those species growing at high altitudes) can therefore be distinguished. We should now enumerate these factors singly.

Just before doing so however, it is important to note that the development of the floral parts can be in the form of a single bloom as in the mountain avens *(Dryas octopetala* and *Geum reptans)* or in the form of a single inflorescence of many small flowers as for instance in the *Saxifragaceae*, the *Umbelliferae* and in many *Compositae*.

In other groups the general increase in both the dimensions and the colour intensity of the floral parts is accompanied by a reduction of the vegetative parts (that is to say the stem and the leaves). In fact, we can often observe, high in the mountains, small, short, prostrate plants, which nevertheless have large blooms or showy inflorescences; examples include *Aster alpinus, Semper-vivum arachnoideum, Primula minima,* various species of the *Gentianaceae (*such as *Gentiana acaulis* and *G. verna)*, *Viola calcarata*, and a lovely carnation, *Dianthus neglectus*, whose corollas often reach a diameter of 25 mm on erect stems which are, themselves, only 25 mm long.

We should also note that plant species common to both the lowlands and high-alpine areas gradually become reduced in size as one rises to higher altitudes. An obvious example is the very common Dandelion *(Taraxacum officinale)* whose flowering shoots can be as tall as 20 cm in the lowlands, shrinking to a mere 2–5 cm in the high mountains. The shoots rise from the centre of circular leaf rosettes, luxuriant growths with diameters of 20–30 cm in lowland or subalpine altitudes, which shrink to diameters of 5–10 cm at altitudes higher than 2,000 m.

As Claude Favarger, the eminent Swiss botanist has said: 'At high altitudes the plant becomes reduced to the blossom, and thus becomes the flower in the triumph of its beauty'.

We might add at this point that, in many cases, the flowers, besides increasing proportionately in size (and often also in number) tend to acquire more intense colour and perfume. For what purpose? We know that the flower is the organ of sexual reproduction equipped to spread fertile pollen on which depends, through pollination, the fertilization of the ovules and the consequent development and ripening of the seeds. We must deduce therefore, that by concentrating all its strength in the flower, the plant attracts the pollinating insects and guarantees survival for the species during its brief existence in the cool, fleeting summer so characteristic of the high Alps.

Another example of alpine adaptation can be found in 'pulverulent' (cushion-like) plants whose vegetative parts are cushion shaped, as found, for instance, in *Silene acaulis*, numerous *Saxifragaceae, Androsace helvetica* and many others.

The cushions are sometimes particularly dense, made up of very short stems, all more or less equal in length, and often sprouting from a common basic rosette to form a semi-circular mass. The stems sometimes appear even more closely packed together, rather like cushions of moss, because of the large number of tiny leaves which cover them. During the brief duration of the fine season, there appear on these green or green-blue cushions (which present a picture of marvellous precision) the hundreds of little flowers which open wide to the rays of the sun and to the bees and insects which are searching for nectar.

We have already referred to the increased intensity of the colours in the flowers of those species of plants which occur in the pastures, ravines and rocky slopes of the high-alpine areas. We must also add that the colours of the alpine flowers are on the whole a different colour, or at least more gaudy and brighter compared to those species found lower down. This phenomenon is undoubtedly an adaptation made in order to be more noticeable to foraging pollinators. Generally, the predominant colours are yellow, pink-purple, white, violet and blue, the latter ranging from intense, cold blues, as in the matchless hues of the gentians to the pastel sky-blue of the forget-me-nots.

Let us now examine a little more closely the vegetative parts of the alpine plants. The stems and leaves are often quite grey or sometimes whitish in appearance, due to a thick tomentum (a dense covering of short, soft hairs). This tomentum is highly functional since it not only protects the delicate parts of the plant from both the intense cold of the freezing nights and from the rays of the sun which are rich in ultra-violet rays, but also provides a means of obtaining water from the atmosphere when the ground is frozen.

The morphology of the vegetative organs of the high-alpine plants offers a surprise inasmuch as

Spring anemone (Pulsatilla vernalis) exemplifies an alpine adaptation to conditions of extreme cold; the flower is very big in proportion to the size of the dwarf vegetative parts (stem and leaves)

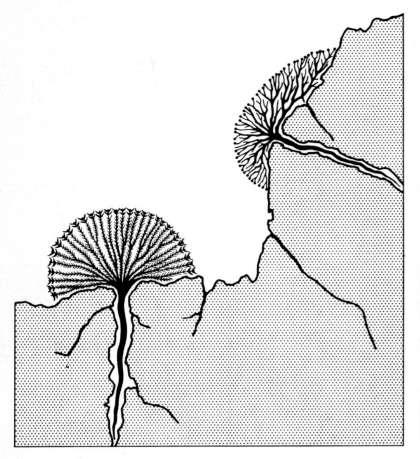

we can see that there is usually a considerable reduction of the epigeal portion (stems and leaves above ground) while there is no corresponding reduction in the hypogeal portion, or root system. In fact here we notice that the tiny plants which grow on rocks and moraines penetrate the cracks between the stones with surprisingly long roots which, try as we may, are often impossible to tear up completely.

The reason why alpine plants tend to develop a long root system into the earth is twofold; not only do they enjoy a wider area of contact between the roots and soil so as to draw up what little water and nutrients there are, but they also anchor themselves more securely to the ground and thus withstand better the forceful mountain winds. It must be remembered that most alpine habitats such as wet cliffs, shingles, moraines, and scree-slopes are constantly being eroded and become extremely insecure. Naturalists generally agree that this combination of reduction in the shoot and vegetative organ and the greater development of the root system (i.e. 'dwarfism') is a key factor for existence and survival in such extreme environmental conditions.

The phenomena of montane adaptations are still more interesting when examined from a physiological viewpoint; this is particularly true of modifications to stem and leaf tissue. Students of plant physiology generally hold the view that

(Above left) This sketch shows how small, cushion-like alpine plants adapt to obtain water and remain attached in extreme, arid and exposed conditions; note how their roots penetrate a long way into the cracks in the rocks

(Above right) A houseleek, Sempervivum grandiflorum. *The succulent leaves and stems are a typical adaptation of alpine plants to xerophytic conditions*

high light intensity slows down the growth of the stems. This is proved by the converse, i.e. by the effect that a lack of light has on plants, which is to make the stems grow exceptionally high. Alpine plants are not only subject to a high light intensity but also experience a relatively short night in comparison with the day. Low night temperatures also inhibit the growth of stems, and all these factors combine to select the obvious and widespread dwarf character in alpine species.

A second fact to be taken into consideration is that, according to Favarger, alpine plants are on the whole over-nourished as a consequence of the high luminosity of the environment which, by favouring the assimilation of carbon by the leaves, results in an excessive production of sugar. This sugar cannot all be converted into starch because of the low night temperatures and so it has to remain in the plant cells. Favarger also explains that the high concentration of sugars determines in turn the more active synthesis of

blue, violet and red pigments, which explains not only the intensity of the flower colours of alpine plants but also the formation of bright pigments that redden the leaves in autumn. Examples of this are presented by a type of bilberry, the Whortleberry *(Vaccinium myrtillus)*, by its marsh relative the Bog whortleberry *(Vaccinium uliginosum)*, by the Alpine bearberry *(Arctostaphylos alpina)*, and by most species of the genus *Sempervivum*.

Finally, the high concentration of sugar and other soluble solids in the cytoplasm encourages greater resistance to the freezing of the cells in winter.

A special kind of adaptation of mountain plants concerns the xerophytic species, or those plants which live in an arid environment, growing on rocks and scree slopes. Some examples of these are the caespitose plants with a very thick cushion and short roots *(Androsace helvetica, Silene acaulis*, etc.). Other plants have a dense, extensive and intricate root system. In both cases, xerophytic plants are capable of retaining considerable quantities of water for a long time.

Some of the better adaptations to xerophytic conditions are shown by the stem and leaf succulents of the genera *Sempervivum* and *Sedum*. The stems and leaves are filled with water whenever it is available, and this provides a suitable means of survival in adverse conditions.

(Above left) Wild pansy (Viola tricolor), *common in stony meadows throughout Europe. In order to attract insects for pollination, the flowers are not only very colourful but are also marked with dark brown streaks radiating from the centre which assist the insects in finding the nectaries. They are called 'nectar lines' or 'nectar guides'*

(Above right) The Whortleberry (Vaccinium myrtillus) *in autumn; the reddening of the leaves is due to pigments formed because of the high concentration of sugars in the leaf cells*

Altitude and vegetation zones

It is easy to understand that in a discussion of alpine vegetation and flora, altitude is a factor of great importance, capable of imposing quite rigid limits on distribution.

It is possible to trace vegetation zones which encircle the mountains, massifs or alpine chains; these zones are defined by their own typical vegetation which can range from different types of woodlands to moorlands, grasslands, and sparse cliff vegetation.

An examination of the vegetation zones soon shows that there are particular sequences of communities in relation to altitude. At lowland levels the predominant woodland vegetation consists of deciduous trees, but these are gradually replaced by conifers in more exposed localities at higher altitudes. Eventually the tree line is reached at an altitude above which only herbaceous plants (alpines) will survive.

It is as well to remember that the upper and lower limits of each vegetation zone vary in altitude as a result of other physical and climatic factors such as latitude and aspect. It is, therefore, obvious that mountain systems remote from one another not only show considerable variations in the floristic composition of their vegetation zones but also show considerable variations of the altitudinal limits of each zone.

As an example, we will categorize the vegetation zones of the European Alpine chain in relation to altitude, starting from the lowlands and working through to the highest peaks. We will distinguish eight zones and discuss them in three sections A, B, and C.

The lowland plains themselves are of little interest to our argument because they are now almost entirely under cultivation by man, and are no longer representative of the characteristic deciduous forests which clad them in the past. We can add that the areas we term as lowlands are now often covered by planted poplar woods and grasslands as well as agricultural and horticultural crops, private gardens, and so on.

Section A The vegetation zones which interest us in the first place are the lowland ones which are together termed foothill vegetation; there are two recognizable zones:

1 The sub-Mediterranean zone, characterized

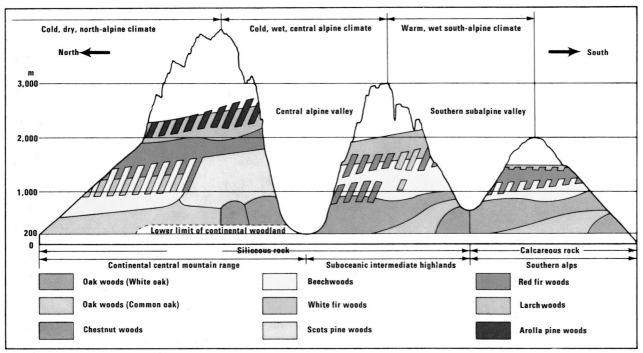

Oak woods (White oak)	Beechwoods	Red fir woods
Oak woods (Common oak)	White fir woods	Larch woods
Chestnut woods	Scots pine woods	Arolla pine woods

(Above) This valley in Lombardy shows the various vegetation zones abruptly changing between the bottom of the valley and the peaks and glaciers. Note that the two slopes, with different aspects, display different physiognomies

by the presence of sclerophyls, or plants with persistent, leathery leaves. This might include the White oak *(Quercus pubescens)* and the Olive *(Olea europea)*, often with different kinds of pines, heathers and brooms; this type of vegetation can be seen all around the Lombard lakes of Northern Italy. This vegetation has a very fragmented distribution on the Alps, and occurs only on the southern slopes. From sea level this zone can rise to between 500 m and 800 m altitude according to the locality. A line marking the extreme upper limit of the sclerophyls is very distinct at these altitudes.

2 The submontane zone, populated chiefly by woods of broadleaved deciduous trees such as oaks, chestnuts, ash-trees, hornbeams, alders, hazels and so on, including, in some cases (according to the degree of exposure) woods of firs and pines. This zone, predominant on northern slopes, also extends from the lowland

plains and reaches an altitude of almost 1,000 m (the upper limit of the oak and chestnut forests).

Section B Immediately above the vegetation of the lowland zone we come to the first of the montane communities, which generally consist of two zones:

3 The lower montane zone is dominated by temperate, deciduous broadleaved trees represented by beechwoods, chestnuts, ash-trees, maples and oaks. Occasionally there may also be pines and firs, particularly the White fir *(Abies alba)*. The upper limit of this zone coincides with a more general one; that of the broadleaved deciduous tree which is at altitudes from about 1,200 m to about 1,800 m. We should note, too, that these mountain woods of temperate broadleaved trees (and especially the beech) occupy cool valleys and slopes whereas on the drier slopes at the same altitude, the woods are generally occupied by evergreens and by the oaks.

15

4 The upper montane zone is characterized by evergreen woods, mostly of conifers with needle-like foliage. Particularly important species are the Red fir *(Picea abies)* and the Larch *(Larix decidua)*, mingled sometimes with Arolla pines *(Pinus cembra)* and in cooler, lower sites, the White fir *(Abies alba)* and in dry exposed ones, the Scots pine *(Pinus silvestris)*. The upper limit of needle-leaved woods more or less coincides with the upper limit of all forestal vegetation, somewhere between 1,600 m and 2,500 m altitude, and generally averaging around 2,000 m above sea level. Where the belt of needle-foliated woods shows its greatest development (as in the central continental sectors of the Alps) it occupies a wide zone which varies in width from about 1,000 m to about 2,600 m; the Red firs and Scots pines are found in the narrower belts joined by Larches and Arolla pines in the wider belts.

Section C At the highest vegetated regions of the Alps is the montane therophyte vegetation which can be broken down into four main zones:

5 The subalpine shrub zone embraces forest and shrubland of various mountain pines including *Pinus mugo* var. *mugo*, stretches of alpine rhododendrons, the Green alder *(Alnus viridis)* and the woody *Vaccinium* shrubs. This type of vegetation has a variable distribution according to the degree of exposure; it descends into the larch and fir woodlands down to altitudes as low as 1,000 m and ascends to beyond 2,000 m.

6 The alpine or upland pasture zone occupies levels above the tree line and the shrub vegetation to beyond 2,500 m altitude. This zone, far from being a continuous cover, because of deep gullies, moraines and scree slopes, may consist of moorlands and low shrubs, as well as pastures covered with flowering species of the *Caryophyllaceae, Cruciferae, Primulaceae, Campanulaceae, Compositae* and the *Orchidaceae*. The homogenous grasslands include many species of the *Gramineae, Cyperaceae* and *Juncaceae* such as mat-grass swards (dominated by *Nardus stricta*), fescue swards (dominated by various species of the genus *Festuca*), and, finally, different forms of wet pastures containing sedges (species of *Carex*) and rushes (species of *Juncus*) as well as other allied species which we have already mentioned.

The alpine pastures and the previously mentioned grasslands which we can define as both steppe and tundra, are often populated, especially in the lower reaches, with several tall plants including very prickly thistles, some gentians, and monkshoods. For convenience we can apply the name megaphorbia to this type of vegetation.

7 At altitudes exceeding 2,500 m the pastureland zone has its upper limit. The vegetation now

consists almost entirely of open or closed grassy turf, and can be termed the high-alpine zone. This pioneer turf vegetation extends in altitude from the lower limit quoted above up to the edge of the perennial snows. Characteristic vegetation includes that dominated by sedges of the genus *Carex*, and dwarf shrubs such as willows (the predominant one generally being *Salix herbacea* which reaches only a few centimetres in height). This zone consists of small, wet valleys between the snow and many high-alpine lakes. The valleys often contain ephemeral forms of vegetation with a large number of mosses and lichens.

8 The snow zone or thallophyte zone occupies both the briefly uncovered snow slopes and the sheer, exposed rock faces at very high altitudes. The latter type of habitat exhibits a characteristic pioneer vegetation with a preponderance of cushion mosses and patches of lichens and algae, which can only be marvelled at for their ability to survive in the face of extreme conditions on the peaks and crags of the high alps, growing as they sometimes do at an altitude of 3,500 m.

The succession of vegetation zones which we have summarized corresponds to what we might observe if we could climb along the slopes of a mountain in the Alpine chain, following an imaginary road.

(Above) View of the vegetation in the Appenines, on a mountain which reaches 1,290 m altitude. The broadleaved deciduous trees thin out on the higher slopes, giving way to pastureland

(Right) On this imposing massif in the Aosta Valley the altitudinal succession of vegetation zones is quite distinct. The upper montane zone of needle-leaved firs and pines is in contact with the subalpine shrub zone and the alpine pasturelands towards the summits. These, in turn, are bounded by snow, though the snow is broken here and there to leave space for pioneer turf

The valley meadows

Reserving a discussion of tropical mountain vegetation for a later part of this book, we will continue to illustrate the plant communities which most frequently occur within the Alpine ranges. To begin our imaginary journey, we shall explore the meadows which stretch almost everywhere along the bottom of the valleys, more or less following the river banks and the spring torrents.

We should ignore those artificial fields which have been sown by man and concentrate on natural grasslands. These original fields, besides containing a large proportion of the *Gramineae*, have a great profusion of plants belonging to many other plant families.

Among the grasses, those which figure largely include Wild oat grass *(Arrhenatherum elatius)*, Cocksfoot *(Dactylis glomerata)*, and the Sweet vernal grass *(Anthoxanthum odoratum)*, a species capable of rising to altitudes of about 2,000 m in the meadows and of penetrating into the woods (especially chestnut groves) at moderate altitudes. In the dryer places are found the Mousetail *(Phleum pratense)* whose long cylindrical spikes justify its name, the Fox-tail *(Alopecurus pratensis)*, the Meadow couch-grass *(Poa pratensis)*, its smaller relative, belonging to the same genus, *Poa trivialis*, the Dog-grass *(Festuca pratensis)*, the Hairy brome grass *(Bromus mollis)*, the Perennial ryegrass *(Lolium perenne)*, and the Yorkshire fog *(Holcus lanatus)*.

Among the common weeds found in the rich meadows, the most frequent are the Dock *(Rumex acetosa)* with its scattered, reddish inflorescences, and the Snakeweed *(Polygonum bistorta)* with its curved roots and thick cylindrical spikes of close-set pink flowers. In the damp meadows we find the widespread *Lychnis floscuculi*, with its pink, notched petals, and its familial relative the Bladder campion *(Silene cucubalus)* with its white flowers, inflated calyces and succulent leaves.

In the meadows we also find an abundance of buttercups *(Ranunculaceae)*, the predominant one being the common Meadow buttercup *(Ranunculus acris)*, which is replaced along the sides of ditches and streams in the generally wetter places by its close relative *Ranunculus repens*, recognized by the less divided leaves.

The *Leguminosae* family are represented by the common Red clover *(Trifolium pratense)*, the White clover *(T. repens)*, the Bird's foot trefoil *(Lotus corniculatus)*, and the Small clover *(Medicago lupulina)*. Often we see the familiar representative of the *Geraniaceae* flourishing in the meadows, the Wood geranium *(Geranium silvaticum)*. Amid the tall plants, smaller ones timidly peep out and show their tiny flowers. Amongst these are the Scarlet pimpernel *(Anagallis arvensis)* with its red and blue petals, the blue-flowered Forget-me-not *(Myosotis palustris)* found in the wetter areas and replaced in dry places by *Myosotis arvensis*, and the pretty Wild pansies *(Viola tricolor)* with their ever variable yellow and violet petals. The *Umbelliferae* certainly do not display such bright colours, although their broad inflorescences can sometimes be showy; common ones include the yellow Parsnip *(Pastinaca sativa)*, the white, Wild carrot *(Daucus carota)*, Wild chervil *(Anthriscus silvestris)* and Sphondilium *(Heracleum sphondylium)* and the white or pink Giant pimpernel *(Pimpinella major)*.

The campanulas, with their big, violet or blue flowers often given *en masse* a particularly blue tone to the meadows; species include *Campanula rhomboidalis, C. glomerata*, with their flowers clustered at the top of the stems, and *C. rotundifolia* with its rounded leaves. There may also be a lot of plantains (of the family *Plantaginaceae*), such as *Plantago lanceolata* which is replaced as one climbs up the grasslands on the slopes by its relatives *Plantago media* and *P. montana*; there may be teasels *(Dipsacaceae)* such as the Wild young widow *(Knautia arvensis)* and the

A meadow in full bloom; the number of different plant species present is clearly indicated by the wonderful range of colours

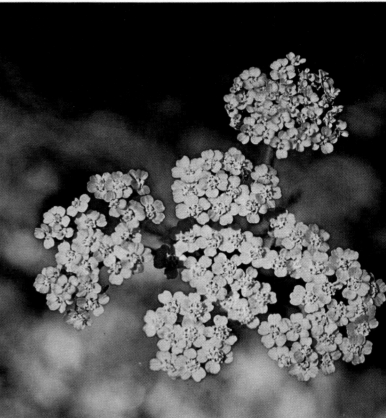

(Above) Two plants
which climb to the
montane zones from the
meadows in the valleys:
the Wood geranium
(Geranium silvaticum)
on the left, and Yarrow
(Achillea millefolium)
on the right

Scabious or Pin-cushion flower *(Scabiosa columbaria)*, both species having compact pink or lilac heads.

There are masses of plants from the mint family *(Labiatae)*; one might see the lovely spikes of violet flowers on the Meadow sage *(Salvia pratensis)* or the small, sky-blue inflorescences of the Bugle *(Ajuga reptans)*. Also one finds the ubiquitous *Compositae* with the Great white marguerite or Ox-eye daisy *(Leucanthemum vulgare)* and the timid Common daisy *(Bellis perennis)*, both species being particularly in evidence in the spring. Quite frequently the meadow is thickly speckled with the bright yellow heads of the Dandelion *(Taraxacum officinale)* at the beginning of spring, accompanied often by *Leontodon hispidus, L. autumnalis* and other, rarer, allied species such as *Tragopogon pratensis* and individuals of the genus *Crepis*. Another common species of the *Compositae* is Yarrow *(Achillea millefolium)* with its small, ivory-white or pink flower heads and its wide flat inflorescence.

Commonly found in these meadows is the Selfheal *(Prunella vulgaris)* with its purple flowers along with the Pyramid bugle *(Ajuga pyramidalis)* with its blue-green or violet tinged, flattened spikes, the yellow Sweet-pea *(Lathyrus pratensis)*, a lovely knapweed with little, pink-lilac heads, *Centaurea jacea*, the small pink century *(Centaurium erythraeum)*, a delicate speedwell with lovely sky-blue flowers *(Veronica chamaedrys)*, *Phyteuma halleri* with its singular clusters of violet-black blooms, the Lady's bedstraw *(Galium verum)* with small, yellow, crossed flowers and the so-called Chicken's milk *(Galium mollugo)* which has white flowers. More unusual are species of the *Liliaceae* such as the Star of Bethlehem *(Ornithogalum umbellatum)* with its white, star-shaped flowers.

We can also find in these magnificent transitional grasslands between the lowlands and the mountain slopes hundreds of other plant species which, though occurring here, are not native. Amongst these is the cosmopolitan St. John's wort *(Hypericum perforatum)* whose latin name reflects a special characteristic – it has leaves which appear to be perforated by a mass of tiny holes when seen against the light.

This type of meadowland belongs to the *Arrhenatherum* community, so-called because of the almost constant presence of the Wild oat grass, *(Arrhenatherum elatius)* to which we have already referred.

The *Arrhenatherum* can rise to between 700 m and 800 m (more rarely to 900 m) with gradual changes in the floristic composition so that new species are added which survive at higher altitudes. At higher altitudes a different type of grassland takes over known as the *Trisetetum* after the dominant component of the community, *Trisetum flavescens*. In both these com-

20

munities the flowers in mid-summer can be seen in their thousands and often include medicinal herbs or those which have edible parts. As two very simple examples we can quote the Dandelion *(Taraxacum officinale)* from which the young leaves of the spring rosettes are gathered, and *Tragopogon pratensis* whose leaves and young roots are used in herbal preparations.

After the summer display, it is common in the meadows to see the feathery down of the thistles, and, from among the flowerless plants, amid the morning mists, come hundreds and hundreds of Autumn crocuses – the poisonous, fragile, *Colchicum autumnale* which announces the beginning of autumn.

We now climb the gentle slopes which stretch up the mountain from the bottom of the valley. Often these grasslands are very extensive, but occasionally they are replaced by oak, chestnut, and ashwoods (higher up by maples and beeches), or, on other occasions there are erratically scattered boulders which have fallen from the mountain tops, typifying the constant erosion of geologically very young mountains like the Alps. Inevitably, the grasslands are destroyed to make way for groups of cottages with whitewashed or grey-stone walls, often encircled by cherry trees in bloom or by hedges and low walls, green with coverings of mosses and ferns.

Here the landscape is less monotonous, punctuated by brooks and waterfalls, by valleys or sunny crags, and often furrowed by mule-tracks and paths.

We have already referred to the grassland com-

munities which extend from between 800 m and 900 m up to between 1,500 m and 1,800 m altitude as the *Trisetetum* communities and we have explained that they are so called because they are dominated by an elegant grass: *Trisetum flavescens*, a plant which in great abundance gives the meadows a golden, picturesque tone. We must add, too, that these communities are largely meadow-pastures, because after the hay harvest, cattle are brought onto them to graze.

Of the plants we have mentioned before some are found more frequently at these altitudes, such as *Leontodon hispidus, Geranium silvaticum, Polygonum bistorta* and *Anthriscus silvestris*. Their abundance often indicates greater or lesser acidity in the soil. In the less acid type of habitat weed species, of the genera *Rumex* and *Polygonum* abound. Weed growth is generally encouraged in these areas by grazing and by man's other farming activities.

At the margin of the woodlands and grasslands, in the so-called ecotone, we find among the taller plants the Mountain buttercup *(Ranunculus montanus)*, the Mountain clover *(Trifolium montanum)*, the Masterwort *(Astrantia major)*, the Meadow-rue *(Thalictrum aquilegifolium)*, a big, yellow flowered cinquefoil *(Potentilla grandiflora)*, the Hairy bellflower *(Campanula barbata)*, often the strongly perfumed White narcissus *(Narcissus poeticus)* and the Cock's crest *(Rhynanthis crista-galli)*, a semi-parasite of the *Scrophulariaceae* with unilaterally arranged yellow flowers which have swollen calyces.

Gradually, as we climb, the lowland plants give

(Below) Two plants common in the meadows: the Meadow clover (Trifolium pratense) *on the left, and the Pyramid bugle* (Ajuga pyramidalis) *on the right*

21

way to more interesting mountain plants such as the poisonous Veratrum *(Veratrum album)* and the Great yellow gentian *(Gentiana lutea)* both with large, ovate-oblong, acute leaves which are so similar that the plants are easily confused. This has frequently led to poisoning in human beings when the large black rhizomes of the Veratrum have been used instead of those of the gentian for making dyes. The veins in the leaves of the Veratrum, however, are completely parallel-ribbed while those of the gentian, if studied against the light, show a fine, reticulate veining. Moreover, the gentian leaves are a brighter, more yellowish green while those of the Veratrum are much darker; there should be no confusion once the two plants are in bloom since the gentian has whorls of large yellow flowers and the Veratrum has greenish flowers on a long spike.

Increasingly common as we climb in the montane meadow-pastures is the Mountain knap-weed *(Centaurea montana)* with its large, branched, blue heads (which are so reminiscent of the Fleur-de-lis), and the Lupin vetch *(Ono-brychis viciaefolia)*, a leguminous plant with clustered pink-lilac flowers. The variety *sativa* is often cultivated as an excellent forage crop.

The hetereogeneity of the landscape allows considerable variation in the flora. In the drier, more exposed, stony places where the soil is less rich in humus we find the lovely plants of the Bugloss *(Echium vulgare)* with its sharp, spiny leaves and stems and blue or reddish flowers. Here, too, we notice the silvery-grey aromatic leaves of the Common wormwood *(Artemisia absinthium)*; this is the herb which plays such an important part in the aromatic flavouring of vermouth. There is the Prickly thistle *(Carlina vulgaris)*, the Verbena *(Verbena officinalis)*, the Feather hyacinth *(Muscari comosum)*, the Bul-bous buttercup *(Ranunculus bulbosus)*, *Hier-acium pilosella*, the Common kidney vetch *(Anthyllis vulneraria)*, and the St. Bernard's lily *(Athericum liliaga)*. Often behind boulders we can catch a glimpse of the silky tufts of the slender Hairy melick grass *(Melica ciliata)* and the ruffled Traveller's joy *(Clematis vitalba)*.

In the very dry places bloom the small, prostrate rock-roses *(Helianthemum vulgare* and *H. chamaecistus)* with their pretty yellow flowers. These plants are often associated with the perf-umed cushions of Wild thyme *(Thymus serpyllum)* which in the driest places often become finely hairy, and *Teucrium montanum*, a prostrate labiate with white flowers.

In the localities where the meadow-pasture is more humid and tends to become marshy, the Arnica or Mountain tobacco *(Arnica montana)*, with its large golden flowers, flourishes. This plant, as will be discussed later, can reach very high altitudes. Also in these localities can be found *Pedicularis sceptum-carolinum* with its rose-pink or violet flowers and helmet-shaped upper petal, the Dropwort *(Filipendula vulgaris)* and the related Meadow-sweet *(Filipendula ulmaria)*, a crucifer with pink-violet blossoms called the Lady's smock *(Cardamine pratensis)*, the flowerless Horse-tail *(Equisetum arvense)*, the Great burnet *(Sanguisorba officinalis)* and,

(Right) White narcissus (Narcissus poeticus) *which can sometimes be prolific in the meadows of the montane zone*

(Below) Two common montane species, found particularly in forest clearings: Thalictrum aquilegifolium *on the left, and* Satureja alpina *on the right*

less frequently found, the lovely blue-flowered Marsh gentian *(Gentiana pneumonanthe)*. The plants which really belong to this well-watered soil are the grasses and foremost among these are *Agrostis alba* and *Molinia caerulea* which flourish in the moorland, and, higher up, the Mat-grass *(Nardus stricta)*.

Among the grasses, orchids, such as *Dactylorchis maculata* with its dark purple speckled leaves, may flower, and there are stretches of the Common cotton grass *Eriophorum angustifolium* with its silky, silver, feathery tufted flowers.

In this sort of environment the mosses begin to abound. Particular inhabitants include species of *Mnium*, *Bryum*, and *Philonotis*, with their small, tight moist cushions. Some are golden, others are emerald green, and they occur in groups and colonies following the rivulets which flow into the rushing waterfalls and rapids.

Even at these altitudes, there remain small centres of human occupation; at one time there were many more of these pleasant hamlets, inhabited by men and domestic animals all the year round.

Nearby stretched the fields of rye and potatoes; two crops which are most suited to the submontane altitudes. Higher up in the mountains it was even sometimes possible to cultivate buckwheat, and the gentle slopes were occasionally adorned with fruit-groves of apples, pears and plums, or even vines.

These days many Alpine villages have become depopulated and the vegetation has suffered as a consequence. The gardens and orchards are deteriorating and weeds have got the upper hand.

This does not mean that the flora is any the less interesting, at least for the naturalist. You can come across the most common weeds which have invaded from the lowlands, such as the wild Barley grass *(Hordeum murinum)* the Sterile brome-grass *(Bromus sterilis)*, the Common nettle *(Urtica dioica)* which is itself often invaded by tangles of a bindweed *(Calystegia sepium)*, the Camomile *(Matricaria recucita)*, the Common thistle *(Cirsium arvense)*, and the Spiny thistle *(Cirsium lanceolatum)*.

Here and there appear colonies of the faintly perfumed Soap-wort *(Saponara officinalis)*, the Yellow melilot *(Melilotus officinalis)*, the Mullein or Aaron's beard with its hairy, golden spikes *(Verbascum thapsus)*, the fragrant Horse-mint *(Mentha arvensis)*, the Common calamint *(Calamintha officinalis)* and the common Fig-wort *(Scrophularia nodosa)*.

Along the lanes and mule-paths reign the ruderal weeds such as the Large plaintain *(Plantago major)*, the Annual poa *(Poa annua)*,

(Above) A lovely plumed knapweed, Centaurea nervosa, *in the stony pastures*

and, on the roadsides, we frequently find the fragrant Origanum *(Origanum vulgare)*, a bindweed, *Convolvulus arvense*, the Dead nettle *(Lamium maculatum)*, and the aromatic, sulphur-coloured Tansy *(Tanacetum vulgare)*.

A special kind of flora enhances the old stone walls of the deserted cottages and the dry-stone walls which follow the mule-tracks; you can see ferns which are normally found higher up on the rocks, like the tiny Wall rue *(Asplenium ruta-muraria)*, the pretty Maidenhair spleenwort *(Asplenium trichomanes)* along with its two related 'northern' species with pinnate fronds called the Forked spleenwort *(Asplenium septentrionale)*, and the Black spleenwort *(Asplenium adiantum-nigrum)*, as well as the Sweet, or Liquorice mountain fern *(Polypodium vulgare)*.

Also attached to walls and rocks is the Rustyback fern *(Ceterach officinarum)*, a strange plant which loves the warmth, together with mosses of the genera *Grimmia* and *Barbula*. Some common succulent plants are found covering stone roofs; these include the Common houseleek *(Sempervivum tectorum)*, the White stonecrop *(Sedum album)* with white or rosy-pink flowers and its close relative, the Rock stonecrop *(Sedum rupestre)* with yellow flowers. Often we meet the dwarf Wild cabbage *(Brassica repanda)*, the Greater celandine *(Chelidonium majus)* which exudes a yellow latex, and the Common pellitory *(Parietaria officinalis)*.

At the foot of low walls we find the little, white, star-shaped flowers of the cosmopolitan Chickweed *(Stellaria media)*, the sky-blue blooms of the precocious Wall speedwell *(Veronica arvensis)* and in the spring the purple-pink flowers of the Dead nettle *(Lamium maculatum)*.

The first woodlands

The lowland woodlands, which rise from the bottom of the valley, are perhaps the most varied on the mountains; they consist of broadleaved deciduous trees ranging from the Sycamore to the Ash, the Hornbeam, the oak and the chestnut. One or the other of these trees establishes itself here and there, depending on the soil conditions, the degree of exposure and the mountain gradient. The Ash and the Sycamore are the most solitary, or, if you like, the least sociable trees, and they space themselves out between Limetrees and Wild cherries. The oak and the chestnut, however, are quite gregarious, tending to grow in groups and so forming distinct types of wood. They are rarely found in isolation, but more often in coppices, just as they can be

seen, for instance, in almost every valley along the entire range of the Alps.

Although we have used the loose term 'oak', we should recognize that there are at least four species of the genus *Quercus* in the Alps.

The first of the four types of oak wood we shall examine consists of the Pedunculate oak (*Quercus pedunculata*). This tree is most often found in the cool, shady, lowland localities but it often rises to greater altitudes along the more shady slopes above the valleys, together with the Black alder (*Alnus glutinosa*) and the False acacia (*Robinia pseudacacia*). This latter tree was introduced into Europe from North America about 200 years ago, and it has invaded large areas of territory, destroying the natural wood-

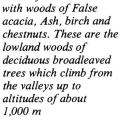

A rocky mountain scene with woods of False acacia, Ash, birch and chestnuts. These are the lowland woods of deciduous broadleaved trees which climb from the valleys up to altitudes of about 1,000 m

On this page are three flowers found in the ground flora of the broadleaved woods. *(Left) Wood anemone* (Anemone nemorosa) *which flowers in early spring. (Bottom left)* Hepatica (Hepatica nobilis) *which flowers in mid-spring.* *(Bottom right)* Primula vulgaris *which flowers in early spring*

Among the plants flowering in the spring we find plenty of Wood anemones *(Anemone nemorosa)*, the pink-flowered Dog's tooth violet *(Erythronium dens-canis)*, sweet blue violets, *Viola odorata*, the paler coloured and inodorous Heath dog violet *(Viola canina)*, the Stemless primrose *(Primula acaulis)*, and many others.

The third type of oak is particularly adapted to the more exposed, sunnier and drier slopes. This woodland consists of the Downy, or White oak *(Quercus pubescens)* recognizable by the down on the lower surface of the leaf and by the fact that the leaves do not fall in winter but become dry and reddish. One can often see this oak in small chestnut woods. It is a much less majestic tree, with its dry foliage among the bare tangle of boughs, than the two oak species we have already mentioned.

The ground flora of the white oak wood does not differ much from that of common oak woodland, but, naturally, the same ecological conditions which have determined the differentiation of the tree communities will also affect the development of the undergrowth. Consequently, we find more plants which like warmth and dryness. Among the shrubs which occur we find the Hazel-nut tree *(Corylus avellana)*, the common Hawthorn *(Crataegus monogyna)*, the Wayfaring tree *(Viburnum lantana)*, the Privet *(Ligustrum vulgare)*, and the Snowy mespilus *(Amelanchier ovalis)*. Of the climbing plants, there is often a profusion of Traveller's joy *(Clematis vitalba)* and the Black bryony *(Tamus communis)*. Among the herbaceous plants we find the Hepatica *(Hepatica nobilis)*, the Wolf's mouth, *(Mellitis melissophyllum)*, sometimes an anemone such as *Pulsatilla halleri*, some geraniums and orchids (which are also common to the oak woods in

(Above) Ash (Fraxinus excelsior), *a cosmopolitan broadleaved tree which grows in the lowlands and often in the mountains, mingling with beeches and sometimes invading the lower conifer woods*

(Right) A snowdrop, Galanthus nivalis, *which grows in the woods and damp meadows up to altitudes over 1,000 m*

land and pioneering dykes and rivers. Although it prefers the lowland habitats it can often climb to about 1,000 m altitude.

The second type of oak wood is definitely the most characteristic along the Alps and is composed of the native European oak *(Quercus petraea)*. This oak wood occurs on the lower slopes of the mountains and is usually heterogenous, including elms *(Ulmus)*, maples *(Acer)*, wild cherry trees *(Prunus)*, Sweet chestnuts *(Castanea sativa)*, and also the Beech *(Fagus silvatica)* on the higher slopes. Its undergrowth is quite rich in flowering shrubs and often ferns too, where there is a stream or a few wet rocks; amongst the shrubs we meet the Alpine buckthorn *(Rhamnus alpinus)*, the Purging blackthorn *(Rhamnus cathartica)*, and brambles like the blackberries *(Rubus fruticosus* and *R. caesius)*.

(Far left) Holly (Ilex aquifolium).
(Left) Yew (Taxus baccata). *Both these trees find shelter in the beechwoods as well as in more open woodland*

(Right) Chestnut groves are among the brighter, more open woodlands; they are often in contact with beechwoods and oak woods

England) as well as field rushes and grasses.

Where the exposure is warmer the White oak is often associated with the Black hornbeam (Ostrya carpinifolia), the Manna ash (Fraxinus ornus), as well as Celtis australis which colonizes rocks often already covered with Ivy (Hedera helix). There can also be a great quantity of Butcher's broom (Ruscus aculeatus) with its lovely red fruit, and the Small-leaved asparagus (Asparagus tenuifolius).

The white oak wood is generally in contact with other tree formations like the sweet chestnut woods and the Scots pine forest (Pinus silvestris) on colder slopes, while on slopes with a different aspect it can be associated with the beechwoods which descend from higher altitudes. On warmer, southerly facing alpine slopes, the white oak wood changes its community characteristics and there are different associated species. For instance, it gives refuge to typically Mediterranean species such as the Holly (Ilex aquifolium) and the Yew, or 'Tree of death' (Taxus baccata). The undergrowth, too, is very varied, containing the Ling or Common heather (Calluna vulgaris) and the more noble Mediterranean Spring heather (Erica carnea) with its little rose-pink flowers, as major components. Both types of heather are, in fact, more frequent in the pinewoods, along with the Box-leaved milkwort (Polygala chamae-buxus).

Finally, the fourth type of oak wood is composed of the Turkey oak (Quercus cerris). Pure stands are not very common or extensive and are generally very similar in appearance to the white oak wood.

Now we can discuss the sweet chestnut woods which, although they are extensive throughout many parts of Europe, are completely unnatural,

(Left) Ling or Common heather (Calluna vulgaris) is an ericaceous heath shrub which often forms pure, or almost pure, stands. It sometimes occurs associated with the ground flora of oak woods, chestnut groves or beechwoods

having been introduced by man from the Iberian peninsula. The predominant European species, the Sweet chestnut (Castanea sativa), is historically well-known. Chestnut woods, which were more extensive and luxuriant in the past, are now seriously undermined by the ink disease, which is due to a fungal infection. There are, however, still chestnut woods and copses to be found everywhere, and they are easily distinguished from other trees by their shiny, serrate, bright-green leaves and, when they are in bloom, by the hanging, finger-shaped, golden male catkins.

The undergrowth of a chestnut wood is rich in varying degrees depending on the amount of light and the characteristics of the soil. In more fertile and cooler places we find the False senna (Coronilla emerus), a few Cytisus species and wide expanses of Whortleberries (Vaccinium myrtillus). Without doubt, however, the most common species of the ground flora are the Common heather (Calluna vulgaris), Bracken (Pteridium aquilinum), and the Snowy woodrush (Luzula nivea), a species which is also often found in the beechwoods. There are many ferns in the cooler spots, such as the Male fern (Dryopteris filix-mas) and the Lady-fern (Athyrium filix-femina).

Amongst the grasses, one finds the Sweet vernal grass (Anthoxanthum odoratum) which enters from surrounding meadows and the Sheep's fescue (Festuca ovina). Many other flowering plants can be found, including the hawkweeds (Hieracium species), the Bishop's wort (Betonica officinalis), and several violets.

Where the soil is poor and more acid we often see copses of Silver birch (Betula pendula) with their white trunks and serrate leaves, the golden-flowered bushes of the Colliers' broom (Sarothamnus scoparius) and thick growths of heather.

Birch trees are always easily recognizable because of their white or silver trunks. They are, as can be seen in this photograph, prolific at the upper margins of the broadleaved woods where the needle-leaved conifers of the montane zone begin to appear

Beechwoods and fir woods

(Below left) A pretty cyclamen (Cyclamen europaea), *this member of the* Primulaceae *with its pink, scented flowers is often found in the beechwoods*

(Below right) An alpine species of foxglove, Digitalis ambigua*; this is a common inhabitant of the Alps at the edges of woodland at altitudes between about 1,200 m and 2,000 m*

The beech has often been called the nobleman of the forest. It is in fact a majestic, elegant tree, with fresh, green leaves throughout most of the year from spring until late summer. In autumn they soon become rust-coloured and fall to the ground where they are extremely persistent and influence the ground flora which can be found in the beechwoods.

At higher altitudes the beechwoods generally succeed the oak and chestnut woods but this does not occur everywhere in the Alps since the beech tree requires a special climate. It needs a shady environment which is neither too warm nor too cold, and neither too dry nor too damp, though it does require a fairly regular water supply. These requirements are the reason that the most luxuriant beechwoods can be found on the exposed northern slopes.

Other factors which determine the growth and development of the beech include wind exposure, soil characteristics, and, recently, man's forestry activities.

The altitudinal limits of the beechwood vary. In Italy, for example, they vary from 450 m to 1,700 m; at the highest known altitudes (between 1,700 m and 1,900 m) it grows in the form of a dwarf bush or shrub.

The undergrowth of the beech tree is not generally very rich, especially where the beechwood is luxuriant. The amount of shade thrown by its elegant, green foliage and the acidic nature of the leaf litter precludes the growth of many other species and it is not unusual to find that in very thick beechwoods the undergrowth is almost entirely confined to small green patches of whortleberries, located wherever the leaf litter is only thin on the ground and a little light can penetrate from above.

Even though they might appear to be completely homogeneous, the beechwoods can differ from one another quite considerably. An example of this variability can be seen, for instance, in a comparison of the beechwoods of the Alpine regions against the magnificent specimens which cover wide expanses of the Apennines and the south of Italy. We should also remember that the beech is very often associated with the White fir *(Abies alba)* because of their similar climatic affinities.

Other trees which are often found with the beech include the Red fir *(Picea abies)*, the Sycamore *(Acer pseudoplatanus)* and the related Norway maple *(Acer platanoides)*. We may also find the Black hornbeam *(Ostrya carpinifolia)* and more rarely the Yew or 'Tree of

flowers with purple patches on the upper petal not found in the second species which grows at higher altitudes among the more typically alpine woods.

The bushes of the undergrowth often include, besides the Whortleberry *(Vaccinium myrtillus)* which we have already mentioned, the Common heather *(Calluna vulgaris)* and the False senna *(Coronilla emerus)* in the poorer, more acid soil. Another striking plant which can easily be recognized is the Spurge laurel *(Daphne laureola)* with its whorled, leathery leaves and the many little black berries which it displays at the end of the summer.

The repertoire of herbaceous plants includes frequent appearances of the Wood sorrel *(Oxalis acetosella)* with its shamrock-like leaves and

(Below left) The Green hellebore (Helleborus viridis), *commonly found in beechwoods*

(Below) Beechwood in spring; notice the persistent carpet of leaf litter

death' *(Taxus baccata)*, the Holly *(Ilex aquifolium)* and even the Larch *(Larix decidua)* at higher altitudes.

We can generalize a little about the undergrowth and mention a few of the more common shrub species, such as the Rowan or Mountain ash *(Sorbus aucuparia)* with its white summer blooms and rich corymbs of globular, red-scarlet berries in autumn, the wide-leaved Priest's hat *(Euonymus latifolius)* with its characteristic four-lobed fruits, and two species of the Medic or Golden rain *(Laburnum anagyroides* and *Laburnum alpinus)*. Both these leguminous species have trifoliate leaves and fine, pendulous bunches of yellow, zygomorphic flowers. The difference between them lies in the fact that the first species, a native to the hill or submontane woods displays

32

violet *(Viola silvestris)*, both the Common and the Whorled Solomon's seals *(Polygonatum odoratum* and *P. verticillatum)* the sunspurges (species of *Euphorbia)*, several Umbellifers including *Sanicula europea*, and an unusual orchid, *Neottia nidus-avis*. The brown colour of this orchid's dry leaves, which lack chlorophyll, and its fleshy, fibred root structure form a mass whose colour and shape give the plant its name of Bird's nest orchid.

Mosses abound in the beechwoods, especially those which prefer cool, shady places like *Mnium undulatum* and *Polytrichum formosum*. Fungi, too, are almost invariably found in abundance and it is possible to distinguish those of the beechwoods which grow on acid soil, from those which prefer calcareous soil. Among the common

pearl-white flowers; the May-lily *(Maianthemum bifolium)* with its numerous small, white flowers, on a stem 5–10 cm in length which can easily be recognized by its two alternate, heart-shaped leaves; the Hepatica, *(Hepatica nobilis)* which has leaves with three lobes and has been given the name Hepatica because the leaves, which are initially green, turn to a reddish-purple, the colour of liver. The Hepatica's pretty flowers consist of six to ten, violet-blue (more rarely purple and white) sepals which both appear and function as petals.

One can also find *Prenanthes purpurea*, the Golden rod *(Solidago virga-aurea)*, the Greater and the Lesser master-worts *(Astrantia major* and *Astrantia minor)*, the Scented woodruff *(Asperula odorata)*, the unscented and pale coloured Wood

species found in acid habitats are the edible *Boletus edulis*, the Cloudy clitocybe *(Clitocybe nebularis)*, *Boletus aereus*, *Tricholoma columbaria*, two more edible *Basidiomycetes*, *Boletus chysenteron* and *B. subtomentosus*, many russulas including the excellent, iridescent *Russula cyanoxanthe* with either a dark green or violet cap, and the unpleasantly bitter *Russula fellea*. We can also occasionally come across the agaric *Amanita excelsa* and some hygrophores.

The poisonous *Boletus satanas* and the lethal *Amanita phalloides* often grow in calcareous, beechwood habitats. In similar localities are the poisonous toadstools *Tricholoma tigrinum*, the Sickener *(Russula emetica)* and *Lactarius chrysorrhoeus*, a sour species with a yellow-coloured latex.

Larchwoods with the Red fir; notice how the larch tends to grow even in the most difficult parts of the mountain

In the conifer woods

Climbing up the mountain slopes, away from the broadleaved woods we come to the narrow-leaved, conifer woods. It is here in these alternately dark and light woods which are always resin-scented, that we really get the feeling of being among mountains. While discussing these conifer woods it is best to note here that they are usually and often erroneously called 'pinewoods'. Pinewoods, however, are strictly speaking woods in which the dominant tree is really a pine (i.e. it belongs to the genus *Pinus*) and the term does not extend to cover woodland composed of Red fir *(Picea abies)* or larchwoods composed of the Larch *(Larix decidua)*.

Conifer woods are so called because they consist entirely of gymnosperm trees reproducing with cones instead of flowers.

The pinewoods of the European Alps are mainly composed of the Scots pine *(Pinus silvestris)*, the Black or Austrian pine *(Pinus nigra)* and the Arolla pine *(Pinus cembra)*. Points of recognition include the fact that the Scots pine and Black pine have leaves formed of needles joined in pairs at their base while the Arolla has them clustered in groups of five. The Scots pine differs from the Black pine in its red bark (the latter has grey-black bark) and its shorter needles which are also considerably lighter in colour.

These three pines occur in very different environments due to the different ecological requirements of each species. The woods of Scots pine are situated mainly on dry, sunny slopes with granitic or siliceous soil; its environmental requirements are different to those of the beech although it often shares the same altitudes. Its undergrowth often resembles a grassland community containing hardy perennial grasses such as *Festuca ovina*. This pine – as we have said before – often invades woods of the White oak, but where it occurs in pure stands (usually on rocky sites) it gives cover to the Juniper *(Juniperus communis)* the Barberry *(Berberis vulgaris)*, the Bearberry *(Arctostaphylos uva-ursi)*, the

Two species common in the sparse Scots pine woods.
(Left) Flowers of the Barberry (Berberis vulgaris).
(Below) Spring heather (Erica carnea)

shelters another well-known parasite, the white-berried Mistletoe *(Viscum album)* known to all for its fruits which are the colour of mother-of-pearl.

The Black or Austrian pine has been used to reafforest some zones of the Alps. It is a conifer of extreme durability, capable of resisting the toughest winter drought conditions.

The Arolla pine – as we shall see later – is associated with the larch at high altitudes. But in the Alps there are plenty of pure stands of *Pinus cembra* and there are noteworthy examples of such stands in the Dolomites.

Forests of Red firs and related trees occupy a great part of the Balkans, central Russia and northern Siberia. On the Alps it is common in eastern and central regions, while in the western Alps, the growth it once enjoyed has been vastly reduced by deforestation. It is, in all events, a characteristic species because of its conical outline, its thick, dark evergreen foliage and its drooping branches, frequently laden with lichens which form long, hanging, glaucous or greyish beards. The dominant species among these lichens include the blackwood beards (species of the genus *Usnea*) or the grey lichens such as *Alectoria jubata* and its allies. Other lichens form clumps on tree trunks, including *Pseudevernia furfuracea*, with a thick thallus divided into a number of lobes which are grey on the upper surface and black underneath, and *Letharia vulpina* which has, by contrast, a lemon-coloured thallus.

The red fir wood copes well enough with

(Above) Scots pine (Pinus silvestris)

(Right) Box-leaved milkwort (Polygala chamaebuxus)*, a characteristic species in pinewoods*

Spring heather *(Erica carnea)*, the Box-leaved milkwort *(Polygala chamaebuxus)* as well as some hardy mosses.

In open, sunny spaces the forest gives way to the growth of several mountain plants; various astragali of the *Leguminosae*, for instance, and particularly the spinose *Astragalus exscapus*; or we see ripples among the golden-plumed Hairy melick grass *(Melica ciliata)*, the silvery plumes of the Feather grass *(Stipa pennata)*, and there may be other grasses such as *Andropogon ischaemon, A. gryllus,* and *Bromus erectus.*

Rock crevices can shelter two interesting ferns with rusty leaves, the Rusty back fern *(Ceterach officinarum)*, and the elegant but rarer *Notholaena marantae*. Elsewhere we find a parasitic flowering plant, the Yellow bird's nest or Dutchman's pipe *(Monotropa hypopithys)*, an unobtrusive species because of its soil-like colour. In the more exposed localities we find the subshrubs of the Rest harrow *(Ononis spinosa)* with its prickly stems and leguminous, pink flowers. The pine foliage often

37

drought and very cold winters as the dry periods are never too long. It generally likes climates which are neither too oceanic nor too warm in summer. It is this conifer wood which is most popularly celebrated in the words and songs of the poets and musicians; 'Siegfried's wood', composed of trees with pillar-like trunks reaching up to the sky. These trees have brown resinous bark, slightly drooping boughs, short, dark green, needle-like leaves which appear rather like a brush on the branches. They are characterized above all by their pendulous, oblong pine-cones which are often very abundant.

The undergrowth of the Red fir is among the most typical and interesting. It is richer in species than any other montane conifer wood, with the exception of the larchwoods, due perhaps to the less dense forest which a larchwood generally develops, so creating lighter and brighter conditions.

In considering the habit of the red fir wood there are three main subspecific distinctions which can be made based on its distribution within the mountain system, its relative altitude (which can vary from approximately 800 m to almost 2,000 m) and finally, the nature of the soil in which it grows, which should be neither too acid nor too alkaline. Naturally the species occurs with a

(Right) The pretty Twin-flower (Linnaea borealis); a tiny plant which grows among mosses and lichens in some Alpine valleys but is much more common in the mountains of north-western Europe and the tundra

(Below) Plants of the Cranberry (Vaccinium vitis-idaea) in fruit; it is frequent in the red fir woods

(Bottom) A variety of V. vitis-idaea in bloom

great number of intermediates, but many valid distinctions can be made on the basis of the composition of the ground flora besides the other characters that we have already mentioned. In the Alps the three main types of fir forest are: the montane red fir wood, which often contains populations of the Beech *(Fagus silvatica)* and White fir *(Abies alba)*; at moderate altitudes we find the transalpine red fir forest, with plenty of bilberries and mosses among the ground flora; finally there are the subalpine red fir woods, which tend to occupy higher altitudes and have bushy undergrowth with a richer herbaceous flora.

In the strange light which illumines a red fir wood there are often plenty of the edible Whortle-berries *(Vaccinium myrtillus)* and the Red cranberry *(V. vitis-idaea)* accompanied by scattered bushes or groups of the Alpenrose rhododendron

(Rhododendron ferrugineum), spinous plants like the Raspberry *(Rubus idaeus)* or the Mountain ash *(Sorbus aucuparia)*, a bush or small tree with red berries which we have already mentioned. Where the soil, even on steep slopes, is left undisturbed it quickly becomes enriched with grasses. Particular species include those of the genus *Festuca* with long, thin almost capillary-like leaves (such as *Festuca ovina* var. *capillata* and *F. ovina* var. *duriuscula*). Among the tufts of these grasses the Wood cow-wheat *(Melampyrum silvaticum)* often occurs with its yellow-white tubular flowers, the whole plant presenting a well-groomed appearance. One also finds a hawkweed, *Hieraceum murorum*, with its yellow heads, and oblong, slightly indented basal leaves which are green on top and often purple-violet on the lower surface. A common orchid which also has its home in this type of wood is the Lesser twayblade *(Listera cordata)* with its thin spike of ivory-coloured flowers, and it is often accompanied by the Hairy bellflower *(Campanula barbata)*, with its distinct, hairy, sky-blue flowers.

Where the soil is very poor and thin, full of boulders, clinging to ravines and to jagged rocks and lined with a layer of dry Conifer needles, a few sparse grasses are the only things that grow, appearing in dried up tufts.

But among and beneath those rocks, in the valleys and ravines, live some very pretty little plants including interesting species like the wintergreens, *Pirola uniflora* and *P. secunda*, the Common speedwell *(Veronica officinalis)*, and the Wedge-leaved saxifrage *(Saxifraga cuneifolia)*.

Both in the mountain systems of north-western Europe and in some localities of the Alpine range

a pretty plant of exceptional delicacy raises its dainty stems and almost circular, notched leaves to remind naturalists of the climatic conditions which prevailed in the remote past during the ice ages. This plant is the Twin-flower *(Linnaea borealis)*, which was named after and dedicated to the Swede, Carl von Linné, who was perhaps the most distinguished botanist of all time. This plant is 5–10 cm in height, and grows between the mosses and lichens on frail, erect stalks, each supporting a couple of bell-shaped white-rosy-pink flowers at the apex.

The red fir wood could perhaps be called the paradise of the Cryptogams. In these woods we find the Clubmoss *(Lycopodium annotinum)* and hundreds of other species of mosses, liverworts, lichens and fungi. There is such a wealth of these flowerless but nonetheless lovely plants that experts lay special emphasis on the red fir woods for conservation. The various species of moss which are among the most abundant include: *Hylocomium splendens* with its elegant, feathery leaves; *Pleurozium schreberi* with its little, purple stems hidden by a thousand tiny leaves; *Ptilidium crista-castrensis*, a delicate species whose leaves become golden and look like miniature ferns; and the common, rather dishevelled *Rhytidiadelphus triquetrus*.

The lichens are innumerable; from those which form cushions which are either dry and rigid or soft and moist (such as the grey-green *Cladonia arbuscula)*, to those which stretch among the mosses to form large expanses of thalli with a leathery look (like *Peltigera canina* and *Peltigera aphthosa)*. These latter species have grey-green thalli which are wide, lobed and sometimes crumpled at the edges, and the fruits of the apothecia rise here and there like small, brown concave flaps. Often there is a great show of lichens with thalli forming small, intermixed colonies called podetia. Examples of lichens which form podetia include *Cladonia pyxidata* with its grey-green trumpet-like structures and *C. bellidiflora* whose podetia bear small, red, enamel-like bodies at their edges.

Fungi in the red fir wood are impressive both for the number of species present and for their sheer abundance. In discussing the fungi forms found in this type of woodland it is reasonable to distinguish those found on acid soil from those growing in calcareous habitats.

Now we come to consider the larchwood whose

The dramatic light in a conifer wood of larches and the Red fir at an altitude of about 2,000 m in a valley of the Eastern Alps

predominant member in the Alps is of course the only native European species of larch, *Larix decidua*. This species is the only conifer in the Alps which sheds its leaves in winter. This is the reason why, in autumn, the golden yellow larch-woods stand out against the grey rocks and the darkly coloured red fir woods.

As we have already mentioned there is a lot of light among the trees of a larchwood and this is due to the relatively uncrowded nature of the individuals, the elegant streamlining of their conical outline, and also the fact that the needle-like leaves are themselves a light green in colour. The leaves can easily be recognized because they are arranged on the branches in loose, circular tufts.

The larch might be considered as *the* alpine tree inasmuch as its presence along the rocky slopes defines the tree line. Small groups of larches or isolated trees can be found up to a maximum altitude of 2,600 m and it can descend to about 100 m.

The optimum range of the larchwood is somewhere between 900 m and 2,200 m altitude. It has a whole range of habit conditions from thick woods to a sparse distribution among grassy, grazed savannas.

The grassy carpet of the undergrowth is, as in the case of the red fir woods, often dominated by *Festuca ovina*, which can be substituted in poorer soil by the Mat-grass *(Nardus stricta)*. The shrub layer includes the lovely Alpenrose *(Rhododendron ferrugineum)*, the Green alder *(Alnus viridis)*, and the dark-blue Honeysuckle *(Lonicera caerulea)*; we also find shrubs, here and there, of the Dwarf juniper *(Juniperus communis var. nana)* and the Common heather *(Calluna vulgaris)*. In more acid soils, we find the thornless Alpine rose with pink-carmine flowers *(Rosa pendulina)*, and the woody Alpine clematis *(Clematis alpina)* with its great, sky-blue flowers. A smaller plant which is often found in extensive colonies is the black-berried Whortleberry *(Vaccinium myrtillus)*. The red Bearberry *(Arctostaphylos uva-ursi)* appears in the drier places and in the more open places we find the fragrant *Daphne striata* with its tufted bunches of rose-pink flowers.

The flowering herbaceous plants grow profusely and are most numerous in the clearings. We can only mention a few here, such as the Great yellow gentian *(Gentiana lutea)* and its sister species, the Spotted gentian *(Gentiana punctata)* and the Purple gentian *(Gentiana purpurea)*. Other common species include the Turk's cap lily *(Lilium martagon)* with its porcelain-like, hanging flowers and recurved petals, the

(Above) Conifer wood of Red fir (Picea abies) *and Larch* (Larix decidua) *in the Aosta Valley. Notice how in autumn the two species are clearly distinguishable since the deciduous Larch becomes a tawny colour*

(Above right) Another example of a conifer wood where some broad-leaved trees are also present

(Above left) Larches (Larix decidua) *with Aspens* (Populus tremula) *and the Wild cherry* (Prunus avium)

(Left) Rocks and rubble, which produce different micro-environments can shelter a number of unusual mountain species

Mountain clover *(Trifolium montanum)*, and the pretty Alpine clover *(Trifolium alpinum)* with its inflorescence of crimson-coloured flowers.

The mosses of the larchwood are, more or less, a repetition of those that can be found in the red fir wood. We can, however, add a few species such as *Polytrichum juniperum* with its dense cushion colonies in which one can count dozens of ochreous little caps which protect and contain the microscopic spores. Wherever there is a moist climate one can also expect to see other moss species of the genera *Bryum, Bartramia, Philonotis* and *Hypnum*.

The lichen flora is also very little different from that of the red fir woods, but in the case of fungi the differentiation between one wood and another is much more noticeable. The variety to be found is even greater if other trees combine with the larch to form a mixed wood. This occurs particularly with the Arolla pine *(Pinus cembra)* which we have briefly discussed already. The dark green Arolla pine is a native of the northern Asiatic mountain regions and probably arrived in the Alps during the ice ages. This majestic tree can – as we have already said – form pure, or almost pure, woods but is often found associated with the larch, thus bringing to the wood a more characteristically Alpine tone. Its colour and

sombre outline, similar to the Red fir, gives the wood itself a more austere character.

There are also characteristic variations of the ground flora, so that the plants we can find in a wood consisting of both larch and Arolla pine include the well-known Twin-flower *(Linnaea borealis)*, the Alpine rock-rose *(Helianthemum alpestris)* and a member of the *Primulaceae, Trientalis europea*, with five or six oblong-pointed leaves arranged like spokes on slender stems, and star-shaped flowers, bearing seven white petals. This last species is quite local and grows in the central and eastern Alps.

We should also remember that while the woods of Scots pine present their own kind of characteristic undergrowth, the undergrowth found among the Red fir, the larch and the Arolla pine woods can have a great deal in common.

It is not impossible for all four of these species of tree to live together with even one or two of them dominating and giving their character to the wood. An obviously rare situation is the cohabitation of the Red fir with the Arolla pine because of the ecological disparities of the two species.

In the ground flora of these mixed conifer woods, we find a number of interesting alpine plants growing together which would normally be separate; for instance, two rhododendrons, *Rhododendron ferrugineum* (which normally prefers siliceous soil, and grows particularly in the western region of the Alps) and *Rhododendron hirsutum* (which prefers calcareous soil, normally in the central and eastern regions of the Alps). In the same way the two bilberries we have frequently mentioned previously can also be found together. Also commonly found in these three conifer woods besides many shrubby and herbaceous species we have already mentioned, is a little, prostrate willow, *Salix reticulata*, the Clubmoss *(Lycopodium selago)*, the Alpine bellflower *(Soldanella alpina)*, *Homogyne alpina*, the wintergreens and many grasses which constitute what we can define as the 'grassy' floor or carpet.

Of the common mosses we can particularly mention *Hylocomium splendens*, *Pleurozium schreberi* and *Rhytidiadelphus triquetrus*, to which we can often add *Polytrichum juniperinum*, *Dicranum scoparium*, *Thuidium recognitum*, and, in very damp places, some peat-mosses of the genus *Sphagnum*.

The lichens include numerous species of *Cladonia*, such as *Cladonia pyxidata* and *C. fimbriata* with elongated, trumpet-shaped structures and teeth all along the edge of its thallus. In amongst the alpine shrubs we find *Cladonia rangiferina*,

C. subulata, C. furcata, C. arbuscula, the Iceland moss *(Cetraria islandica)*, *Peltigera canina* and *P. aphthosa* as well as various species of *Parmelia*. Shaded, rotten tree stumps and rocks are often splashed with the dusty thalli of powdery lichens. The most frequent species include *Lepraria aeruginosa* which is grey-glaucous in appearance, and *L. candelaris*, which is sulphur yellow

(Above) Prostrate bushes of the Dwarf juniper (Juniperus communis var. nana) on rocks

(Above) Three species frequently found in the meadows at the level of the larchwoods.
(Left) Spotted gentian (Gentiana punctata).
(Centre) St. Bruno's lily (Paradisia liliastrum).
(Right) Turk's cap lily (Lilium martagon)

(Left) Larchwoods can often assume the appearance of a cultivated park until their undergrowth becomes considerably richer with many herbaceous species

(Right) Example of the Arolla pine (Pinus cembra) in its usual rocky environment

At the edges of conifer woods

The conifer woods, depending on the degree of exposure and the particular habitat which they occupy, form the greater part of the montane zone. They also extend to the higher altitudes to form the tree line at the subalpine level.

The altitudinal belt which they occupy is often very wide and, as one can see, presents one of the most structurally heterogeneous vegetation zones. Thus, it is possible to find, within the zone, naked, precipitous rocks and shattered boulders, ranging from gigantic monoliths to the small stones found in areas of landslides or moraines. Yet one can also find vertical ravines or expanses of sloping cliff-face where an appreciable layer of earth has been able to cover the rock.

It is natural, then, that where the wood has not been able to establish itself, or where it has been eliminated by man during his work of destruction there should be a great variety of vegetative associations.

So, let us turn from the conifers to admire the pasture-meadows (i.e. meadows that can be harvested and grazed) which are so often bathed in sunlight. Each successive season brings a different appearance to these grasslands which appear between the woodlands. As the winter snows melt, the crocuses (such as *Crocus vernus*) begin to peep out in thousands from the damp, bare soil. Their tapered, white or violet flowers are closed at first, but then the six petals open to reveal the golden anthers.

Among the plants which come later we find the timid Common daisy *(Bellis perennis)*, Meadow clover *(Trifolium pratense)* which at these altitudes appears as a pale-coloured variety (var. *nivale*), the Lady's mantle *(Alchemilla vulgaris)* with leaves that have rounded lobes and serrated edges, a hawkweed *(Leontodon autumnalis)*, the Wild pansy *(Viola tricolor)* and many other dwarfed species of the genera *Trifolium, Leontodon, Euphrasia* and *Campanula*. These species often end up being hidden by the more vigorous summer plants which are taller and more prolific. A great number of them have risen to the alpine pastures from the lowland meadows and valley bottoms and amongst these we find the Cocksfoot *(Dactylis glomerata)*, the Sweet vernal grass *(Anthoxanthum odoratum)*, the Dock *(Rumex acetosa)*, the Snakeweed *(Polygonum bistorta)*, the large white Marguerite *(Leucanthemum vulgare)*, various violet campanulas, (such as *Campanula glomerata, C. barbata, C. rhomboidalis,* and *C. scheuchzeri)*, the Wild young widow *(Knautia arvensis)*, and the Small scabious *(Scabiosa columbaria)*.

The high grasslands are a meeting place for a thousand colours; there are the yellow-golden heads of *Arnica montana* and some *Doronicum* species (which also occur on the pastures at higher altitudes), the swollen, yellow flowers of *Rhynanthus crista-galli*, the opaque, hairy inflorescences of *Anthyllis vulneraria*, and the greenish spray of blooms of *Veratrum album*.

The grasslands can also take on very different appearances owing to the variety of plants which brighten them at various times in mid-summer. There are a number of cases when just one species predominates and gives the grassland its own particular colour. It may be the fragrant White narcissus *(Narcissus poeticus)* which, rising from the valley finds its highest possible habitat in the alpine grasslands, or the golden Globe flower *(Trollius europaeus)* or perhaps more rarely the red or yellow Southern tulip *(Tulipa australis)*. The more common Meadow sage *(Salvia pratensis)* can dominate the colouring with its amethyst spikes as can the blue or yellow columbines *(Aquilegia* species*)*. Among the most beautiful flowers to adorn these meadows are, without doubt, the anemones such as the White alpine anemone *(Pulsatilla alpina)* and its yellow relative *P. alpina* subsp. *apiifolia*.

Also at the level of the conifer forests there is often much poorer soil where the land is so flat that it retains water and is consequently permanently damp. This is where the Mat-grass *(Nardus stricta)* grows in a hairy, greyish, herbaceous carpet which, in some ways, is reminiscent of the Asian steppe lands, whilst in other ways it can recall the look of an Arctic tundra.

Flowering Spring crocuses (Crocus vernus)*; the snow has just melted at the foot of a wood of Larches and Red firs*

The absolute dominance of the hardy Mat-grass is due to its ability to resist both drought and protracted humidity. This grassland is often considered to be quite insignificant and sad, but there are times when here too a startling splash of colour will brighten the landscape.

In fact, besides other grasses such as *Phleum alpinum, Festuca halleri, Festuca rubra, Deschampsia flexuosa, Agrostis alba, Poa alpina, Anthoxanthum odoratum* and rushes belonging to the *Juncaceae* (e.g. *Luzula campestris* and *Luzula lutea*) which all appear among the Mat-grass, there are other plants with bright flowers like the modest yellow flowered Tormentil *(Potentilla erecta)*, the Pyrenean hawkweed *(Leontodon pyrenaicus)*, the related Hairy hawkweed *(L. hispidus)*, the eye-brights, plants sometimes so small that they escape attention, (such as *Euphrasia officinalis, E. alpina* and *E. minima*), the Mountain buttercup *(Ranunculus montanus)*, the white Pennywort *(Thlaspi alpestre)*, *Antennaria dioica*, a hairy plant with white or rose-pink heads, the violet Felwort *(Gentianella amarella)*, a carnation, *Dianthus alpestre*, an orchid with speckled leaves, *Dactylorchis maculata*, the so-called Mountain vanilla *(Nigritella nigra)*, some lichens, including the Iceland moss *(Cetraria islandica)* and the Reindeer lichen *(Cladonia rangiferina)* as well as a great variety of mosses.

Often the Mat-grass is scattered with rocks up against which higher plants and bushes grow, such as the Raspberry *(Rubus idaeus)*, the Dwarf juniper, *(Juniperus communis* var. *nana)* or the Barberry *(Berberis vulgaris)*. It can sometimes be patchworked with green expanses of bilberries *(Vaccinium* species*)* and heather *(Calluna* and *Erica* species) which in autumn is covered with

(Above) Examples of larchwoods, alpine pastures and shrub-covered rocks at the top of the Aosta Valley

rose-lilac flowers in tight, neat spikes.

From these types of Mat-grass communities it is only a short step to the heathland; in fact, the soil may be so poor that it is only really suited to heather growth. The heather soon becomes dominated by Ling or Common heather *(Calluna vulgaris)*. The prolific heather growth restricts the development of other plants and, consequently, the accompanying flora becomes very poor, often limited to the presence of a few grasses such as the Blue moorgrass *(Molinia caerulea)* and White bent *(Agrostis alba)*, with some herbaceous plants which we have already mentioned like the Tormentil *(Potentilla erecta)*, a few rock-roses (species of *Helianthemum*) and others like the Purple-flowered milkwort *(Polygala vulgaris)*, the White-flowered cinquefoil *(Potentilla alba)*, and the Montane sheepsbit *(Jasione montana)*.

We should now examine a rocky environment, and picture ourselves enclosed by meadows on one side, and by conifers (most typically the larchwood) high up on the other. The scene is dominated by rocks, which are scattered around or piled up as though they had been playthings in the powerful arms of a giant, creating a chaotic landscape. A large boulder might tower well above the other rocks, and be completely covered in lichens; the species belonging to a number of genera such as *Verrucaria, Caloplaca* and *Physcia* with reddish thalli, and *Umbilicaria pustulata* with dry, grey, leaf-like thalli, which, as the name implies, are peppered all over with little black pustules.

The mosses found on the rock are in the form of grey or black cushions and normally belong to the genera *Grimmia* and *Schistidium*. These genera are sometimes associated with *Rhacomi-*

Some characteristic flowers at the level of the conifer woods.
(Top left) Euphrasia officinalis.
(Top right) Campanula barbata.
(Below left) Anthyllis vulneraria.
(Below right) Campanula scheuchzeri

49

Veratrum album, *a herbaceous plant of considerable size, common in the grasslands near the conifer woods; this is a plant whose poisonous rhizome is often confused with that of the Great yellow gentian*

trium and some pleurocarpous groups such as *Dicranum.*

Under the boulder, which provides shelter, shade and coolness, we find the Yellow wood violet *(Viola biflora)* displaying the pairs of little yellow flowers which each of its delicate stems supports. Still further into the shade, where there is almost constantly dripping water, we can easily recognize the alternate, round, green-yellow leaves of the Golden saxifrage *(Chrysosplenium alternifolium).*

Here, too, we find the ideal environment for ferns; indeed, in the cracks of the great boulder, polished and rounded by time and weather, in the thin but adequate soil, are little plants of the Wall rue *(Asplenium ruta-muraria).* With it we might find four other related species: firstly, the Maidenhair spleenwort *(Asplenium trichomanes),* with its tiny, elegant pinnate lobes inserted as

sub-opposite pairs on a common, shining black rhachis, very reminiscent of the Maidenhair fern *(Adiantum capillus-veneris)*; secondly, the Forked spleenwort *(Asplenium septentrionale)* with its very narrow, forked leaves; thirdly, but more rarely, the Green spleenwort *(Asplenium viride)*; lastly, the Black spleenwort *(A. mifrum)* with its wider, dentate, leathery lobes and with a brown-black rhachis towards the base. We can also find these species quite often growing in dry-stone walls which separate the plots of cultivated land from the alpine pastures.

Some other ferns found in this environment include the Brittle bladder fern *(Cystoperis fragilis)* with its delicately divided leaves; the False liquorice *(Polypodium vulgare)* with its sickly sweet rhizome, which we have already met on the rocks among the chestnut woods; *Polypodium drypopteris* with its fine, tripinnate leaves;

Polystichum lonchitis with its long, pinnate leaves divided almost completely into rather sickle-shaped and denticulate triangular segments. Sometimes we find the Male fern (*Dryopteris filix-mas*) and the Lady fern (*Athyrium filix-femina*) in the coolest, most humid places, and among the rocks and ruins exposed to the sun we might see the green clumps of the Parsley fern (*Cryptogramma crispa*) whose finely divided fertile pinnae are much longer than its triangular, sterile ones.

On the rocks, however, there are not only the ferns and the other few plants we have already mentioned. In the warm, more exposed positions, we find the succulent alpine plants with their fleshy leaves and stems such as the stonecrops (*Sedum* species) to which we have already referred. Among the more common species we find some with white flowers such as the White stonecrop (*Sedum album*) and others with yellow flowers such as *Sedum sexangulare* and the more luxuriant Rock stonecrop (*Sedum rupestre*).

Also in this type of habitat we find the houseleeks (*Sempervivum* species) with their characteristic basal rosettes of overlapping leaves. There are three common species: the Common houseleek (*Sempervivum tectorum*) and the Mountain houseleek (*S. montanum*), which both have dark red or purple flowers, and the elegant, decorative Cobweb houseleek (*S. arachnoideum*), with its basal rosettes of small leaves covered with long, white matted hairs, and with fragile stems supporting one or more star-shaped flowers of a remarkable, intense, purple colour. A related species, with yellow flowers, is *Sempervivum wulfenii* which grows in the stony alpine pasture-lands or on gravel among clumps of grasses.

A fairly rare rock plant found on the steep slopes is the Pyramidal saxifrage (*Saxifraga cotyledon*) with its large basal rosettes of rigid, strap-like leaves from which rises a long, plume-like spray of small white flowers. A much more common montane saxifrage is one of the smaller species, the Livelong saxifrage (*S. paniculata*).

Outside the conifer woods, in the grassy plateaux where the ground may dip slightly to form hollows, marshes are often formed. As in other wet places, or at least very humid grasslands, the marshes show their nature not only by the flora which characterize them but by the successive stages through which they pass from their non-marshy edges to the slight central depressions where the presence of water is more constant.

Around the marsh are numerous species of sedges and rushes of the genera *Carex, Cyperus*

Red elder (Sambucus racemosa) *is a shrub commonly found at the edge of the conifer woods. The illustration on the left shows the whole plant while the one above shows a bunch of its berries*

and *Juncus* among which stand out the heads of the Arnica *(Arnica montana)*, and golden flowers of the Globe flower *(Trollius europaeus)*. Here and there clumps of two common marsh grasses, the Purple moor grass *(Molinia caerulea)* and the Median quaking grass *(Briza media)* interrupt the homogeneous, waving display of the narrow-leaved Cotton grass *(Eriophorum angustifolium)*. Among the more attractive flowers we find an orchid which we have already mentioned – the Spotted orchid *(Dactylorchis maculata)*, as well as the white Grass of Parnassus *(Parnassia palustris)*, the Tormentil *(Potentilla erecta)*, *Tofieldia calyculata*, the blue-flowered Felwort *Gentianella amarella*, and low bushes of heather and bilberry among the tall, thin plants of the Field thistle *(Cirsium palustre)*, with its crimson-purple heads.

Quite often in the marshland we can catch glimpses of rivulets hidden between banks of emerald-green mosses; especially *Philonotis fontana, Cratoneuron commutatum* and the golden or copper-coloured, spongy stretches of peat-moss *(Sphagnum* species*)*. There is often a wonderful show of the Marsh marigold or Kingcup *(Caltha palustris)*, a member of the buttercup family with large, orange-yellow flowers. Among its luxuriant clumps peep out the white, four-petalled flowers of the various species of *Cardamine*, the Rockcress *(Arabis bellidifolia)*, as well as the minute, pink flowers of the delightful Bird's-eye primrose *(Primula farinosa)*. We also

quite often see the Alpine willowherb *(Epilobium alsinifolium)*, the Starry saxifrage *(Saxifraga stellaris)* with its small, white flowers, and the related Yellow mountain saxifrage, *(Saxifraga aizoides)* which is also found in high pastures.

If the marsh is near a wood or contains a few rocks so that areas of shade are provided it more often shelters various species of butterbur *(Petasites officinalis, P. albus* and *P. paradoxus)* with their tufted heads of snowy white or reddish flowers and their big, fleshy, round-lobed, dentate leaves. One might also find *Adenostyles glabra*, among which hide plants of *Saxifraga stellaris* and *Veronica beccabunga* with its sky-blue flowers.

The rivulets gradually become wider and their banks are cluttered with stones. As they descend their course becomes increasingly tortuous, developing into rushing, gurgling cascades and rapids, whose clear, cold waters are so refreshingly pure to drink. Reflected in these racing waters, caught against the cobalt sky we might see the rose-crimson flowers of the Red stonecrop *(Sedum roseum)*, or the blue flowers of the bellflowers *(Campanula* species*)*. At the edge of the stream between the grasses and the dry stones, the tall plumes of the Rose bay willowherb *(Epilobium angustifolium)* among young birches, thorny barberries, raspberries and high bushes of Red elder *(Sambucus racemosa)*, a species which is more red than green in the autumn because of the abundance of its scarlet berries.

Rhododendrons and other dwarf shrubs

At the upper extent of the larch and the arolla pine woods the woodland reaches its upper limits. Beyond these limits stretch pastures or wide expanses of alpine scrub consisting of twisted shrubs, the Mountain pine, Green alder and rhododendrons.

Often this vegetation is closely allied to the conifer woods and therefore the two communities can often be seen to merge with one another.

The Mountain pine *(Pinus mugo)* is one of the principal components of this new scene; it can exist as an erect tree, a large bush, or it can even become completely prostrate, with curved boughs originating from a twisted, creeping trunk and closely clinging to the outline of the rocks.

Botanists distinguish three varieties of this conifer, on the basis of the shape of the pine cones and the woody scales which constitute them. The chief variety of the Mountain pine is *Pinus mugo* var. *mugo* which is to be found in crags and calcareous, rocky scree slopes (especially in the eastern Alps). The second variety, var. *rostrata*, grows in stony places and scree slopes on granitic or siliceous soils in the western Alps. The third, var. *pumilio*, is a hybrid of the other varieties, a sprawling shrub which belongs to the mountains of central and southern Italy, and to the central and eastern Alps.

Often these pines form intricate, pioneer woodlands whose open clearings frequently shelter other mountain shrubs such as the Spring heather *(Erica carnea)* or, in other cases, the Savine juniper *(Juniperus sabina)* and the Dwarf juniper *(Juniperus communis* var. *nana)*.

A plant with a similar stature, but occurring in very different environments is the Green alder *(Alnus viridis)*, a shrub which can reach 5–8 m in height and mingle along the paths of the brooks

(Below) An Alpenrose rhododendron in bloom (Rhododendron ferrugineum)

(Below right) Flowering plants of a common monkshood, Aconitum napellus, *a poisonous herbaceous perennial which can be found at the level of the rhododendron shrubs*

Dwarf juniper shrub growing against a rock (Juniperus communis *var.* nana)

and waterfalls at lower altitudes, with the common Black alder *(Alnus glutinosa)*. It differs from *A. glutinosa* mainly because of its finely denticulated leaves. When in its ideal environment, which is along the streams that flow down from the snowfields along the steep slopes and crags of siliceous rocks, the Green alder often forms intricate and tangled thickets of considerable size which merge into the conifer woodlands or even thin out into pasturelands. Amid the leaping waters of the streams, the Green alder creeps between the rocks, keeping them in place and allowing several herbaceous plants to live and flourish, such as the Golden rod *(Solidago virga-aurea)*, the Blue sow thistle *(Cicerbita alpina)* with its light blue heads, the related, dark-blue-flowered *Prenanthes purpurea*, and the monkshoods or wolfbanes, with their spikes of yellowish (in the case of *Aconitum lycoctonum)* or violet-blue flowers (in *A. napellus* and *A. paniculatum)*.

Where the shrubs are thinner, and the water is slower running, the Coltsfoot *(Tussilago farfara)* returns, together with the purple-spiked willow-herbs *(Epibolium* species*)*, the Lady's smock *(Cardamine pratense)* and the ferns, all found among the moist cushions of emerald-green mosses.

But one of the most striking, showy and interesting Alpine woodlands, rich with purple flowers in mid-summer, is the one consisting of the 'Alpenroses' *(Rhododendron* species*)*. At this point we must distinguish between the two mountain species of this genus which are very much admired and collected. The first one is the typical Alpenrose *(Rhododendron ferrugineum)* with its leathery, lanceolate leaves which are green and shining on the upper surface and are

dull and rust-coloured underneath; this species is found along the whole Alpine range, but it is especially common in the western Alps. The second species, a little less robust than the first, is the Hairy Alpenrose *(Rhododendron hirsutum)*; the leaves in this species are not rust-coloured underneath but are bright green on both sides and are hairy along the margins. *R. hirsutum* is a very distinct species and is limited to the central and eastern European Alps.

As well as forming pure stands, the rhododendrons also invade the larch and fir woodlands, sometimes even descending as far as the beech-woods and the chestnut woods. Generally, however, as we have said, they occupy the dry, rocky crags beyond the tree line, where they pioneer the high-alpine screes and rubble.

The *Rodoretum* (a name often applied to the rhododendron community) often provides a link between two different types of alpine vegetation: that found among rocky crags and ravines and that of the alpine pastureland. This is the reason why, despite its apparent homogeneity, the *Rodoretum* shelters, in the clearer patches, shrubs and herbaceous plants characteristic to both environments. For example, here and there stretch broad patches of the Bearberry *(Arctostaphylos uva-ursi)*, the Raspberry *(Rubus idaeus)*, the clubmosses *(Lycopodium clavatum* and *L. alpinum)*, clumps of grasses, the Arnica *(Arnica montana)*, and the Great yellow gentian *(Gentiana lutea)*.

A plant which is often found associated with the rhododendrons is the Dwarf juniper *(Juniperus communis* var. *nana)* which varies in form from low, round bushes to small, prostrate, untidy clusters. It has small, rigid and prickly leaves and fragrant, blue-black berries.

(Left) Rhododendron bushes in flower near pastures on the Dolomites whose impressive peaks form a wonderful backdrop

Xerothermic oases

By xerothermic oases we mean a type of environment which covers a limited area, and is characterized, apart from its altitude, by a generally warm, dry climate dependent on a certain degree of exposure to the sun and a low rainfall.

These oases are found scattered along the whole of the European Alpine range, as well as in other mountain systems. They remain as floral relics of past climatic periods which favoured the expansion of particular vegetation types, mostly of Asiatic steppe origin. Thanks to the location of these 'oases' the Asiatic relics have managed to survive up to the present day.

These localities give refuge above all to a number of grasses *(Gramineae)* of steppe origin of the genera *Stipa, Chrysopogon, Andropogon,* *Bromus,* and *Avena.* We also notice, of course, an abundance of xerophytes. There are species representing many families including the *Cariophyllaceae,* the *Compositae,* the *Labiatae* and the *Umbelliferae.* We often find bushes of the Common juniper, stretches of tangled briars and the thorny barberries. Frequently also present are the various cushion mosses of the genera *Grimmia, Schistidium, Tortella,* and *Trichostomum.*

Turning to actual examples of xerothermic oases we can find several instances worth examination in the European Alps of which we will select just one which occurs in the Dora Baltea Valley, a part of the Aosta Valley.

The oases of the Aosta Valley have a definite steppe-like appearance; they occupy the rocky

An example of a xerothermic oasis in Piedmont. Prostrate plants of the Wild prickly pear (Opuntia vulgaris) *can be seen on the rocks*

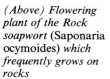

(Above) Flowering plant of the Rock soapwort (Saponaria ocymoides) *which frequently grows on rocks*

(Above right) Flowers of the Red campion (Silene dioica), *a species common at the edge of mountain woods*

(Right) Sedum album and various mosses

slopes with a southern exposure. In them survive the Common thyme *(Thymus vulgaris)*, a typically Mediterranean plant which, in fact, is frequent along the western Italian coast. There are some grasses of central Asiatic steppe origin such as the Feather grass *(Stipa pennata)* and its close relative *Stipa capillata,* the Hairy melick grass *(Melica ciliata)* with its silky-golden spikes, and the very slender *Koeleria valesiana.* Of the *Compositae* we find two wormwoods *(Artemisia campestris* and *A. valesiaca)*, and *Xerathemum inapterum* with its rose-pink, dry heads, a plant which still survives in eastern Europe (where it originated) and which has also become common in the warm regions of the Mediterranean countries.

Of the *Umbelliferae* we find *Eryngium campestre*, and the *Cruciferae* are represented by *Alyssum alyssoides.* Also present is a rare plant of the *Caryophyllacaeae, Telephium imperati.* Lastly we can name two other plants from the eastern Asian steppes, *Kochia prostrata* and *Salsola kali* (both members of the *Chenopodiaceae*). This short, scrub vegetation which is so unostentatious, is broken here and there by bushes of the Etruscan honeysuckle *(Lonicera etrusca)*, which has recently become the object of conservation in Italy.

Xerophytic grasslands

From the xerothermic oases to the xerophytic grasslands is a short step. This term again refers to a 'xeric' type of vegetation (i.e. one found in a warm, arid climate), but in this case it is vegetation consisting almost entirely of species of the *Gramineae*.

The xerophytic grasslands occupy well exposed, sunlit slopes both at the level of the woodlands of broadleaved, deciduous trees, and higher up, until they merge into the shrub layer of the dry rocks, where we find the Barberry *(Berberis vulgaris)*, the Sloe, *(Prunus spinosa)*, the Gooseberry *(Ribes grossularia)* and the Common wormwood *(Artemesia absinthium)*.

The predominant grasses include species of the genus *Bromus* (such as *B. erectus*), the Hairy melick grass *(Melica ciliata)*, *Andropogon gryllus* and *A. ischaemon*, the viviparous form of *Poa bulbosa*, and the Feather grass *(Stipa pennata)*. In addition to these grasses there are a number of species belonging to other plant families. From the *Compositae* we find *Carlina vulgaris*, *Artemisia campestris*, *A. absinthium*, and the thistles such as *Onopordon acantium*, *Cirsium lanceolatum* and *C. arvense*. There are knapweeds such as *Centaurea solstitialis*, *C. calcitrapa*, and *C. maculata*, and legumes *(Leguminosae)* such as *Melilotus officinalis* and *Medicago minima*.

Each plant adds to the aspect of the landscape which repeats, in miniature, those windy, immense, frighteningly lonely and monotonous Asiatic steppes.

(Below) Example of steppe vegetation with a large colony of Common wormwood (Artemisia absinthium)

Alpine pasturelands

We have finally reached the true realm of the mountain flowers, the alpine pasturelands which every summer display thousands of different blooms. Here, too, we find the aromatic herbs whose many medicinal properties have almost been forgotten; both their aesthetic and therapeutic values, once so highly prized, are now often ignored.

On these pastures feed the flocks of sheep and the cattle herds. The soft sounds of cowbells travel far over the otherwise silent grasslands through the fresh, clean air. Few people can visit the pastureland without a feeling of invigoration; at these heights the sun seems brighter, the water clearer and life healthier than in the lowlands, among the urban sprawls with their pollution

(Below) Where the conifers are much thinner, there are wide areas of rocky hillsides suitable for pasturelands

problems, the frantic pace and overcrowded, almost claustrophobic streets.

And yet this aspect of the mountains, the peace and the intoxicating clarity, is becoming fast more difficult to find. Among the most inspiring of engineering feats have been the tunnels and the ramparts, the great columns of steel and concrete on which a highway of several lanes seems to balance gracefully, and almost precariously, on its way to the passes. Inevitably, long chains of automobiles climb along these giant roads, bringing noise and fumes. All too often the visitor finds it convenient to travel in this way, stopping along the wayside and seeing only those areas which have been affected by man. The best, and obviously the most natural way to see the

alpine pastures and to admire the multitude of miniature beauties which they offer, is simply to take a walk.

The population of the mountain districts is changing too. As in so many other areas the native population is diminishing and the transient, visiting population from the cities is increasing. This may sound a little depressing but we should remember that mountains are, by their nature, vast, and it has not yet become too difficult to walk alone, to gaze over enormous distances and see no-one; such solitude, amid the fragrant air and the dancing colours, is something which everyone should experience at some time in their lives.

The alpine pastures are an immense carpet covering all types of rocks and soil. The pastures on limestone rocks which we find, for instance, among the Dolomite peaks, are often dominated by a modest pioneering grass, the Blue sesleria (*Sesleria caerulea*). This species is often associated with sedges of the genus *Carex* which grow thicker wherever the soil is wetter and richer in humus.

These patches of green carpet ripple in the wind among the grey stones and rocks and boast many wonderful flowers such as the Golden and Spring cinquefoils (*Potentilla aurea* and *P. tabernaemontani*); the common Buckler mustard (*Biscutella leavigata*) with its small, yellow, clustered flowers and its unmistakable, characteristic fruit which are small siliquas composed of

Some plants of the Alpine rocky slopes. (Top left) Alpine eryngo (Eryngium alpinum). *(Top right) Aster alpinus. (Below left) Tuft of* Biscutella laevigata. *(Below right) Group of Edelweiss* (Leontopodium alpinum)

(Above) Haller's anemone (Pulsatilla halleri)

two flattened, slightly convex discs, coupled side by side; the attractive White alpine anemone *(Pulsatilla alpina)*; the Purple gentian *(Gentiana purpurea)* with its swollen, purple-red flowers clustered together in the axils of the leaves; the Alpine kidney vetch *(Anthyllis vulneraria* subsp. *alpestris)* with gold-yellow flowers, often tinged with white and red at the tips of the petals and grouped together in globose heads; the Alpine aster *(Aster alpinus)* a species related to the common Michaelmas daisy which has brilliant, violet-blue outer petals and is often associated with the Long-spurred pansy *(Viola calcarata)*, a honey-fragrant plant with violet to pink pastel flowers, which can sometimes be yellow, and, more rarely, white.

In some parts of the calcareous Alps, in the stony pastures between 1,500 m and 2,500 m altitude we can sometimes find the Alpine and Silver eryngos *(Eryngium alpinum* and *E. spina-alba)*; these are species of the *Umbelliferae* whose inflorescences, with globose or oblong heads, are crowned by long, narrow, spine-toothed bracts, dark or light blue in colour, which descend onto the stem to form elegant whorls or verticills.

Also in the pastures on limestone rock one of the most common plants is the Alpine star or the Edelweiss *(Leontopodium alpinum)*, a species which prefers to climb onto the rocks, among the fescue swards and the prostrate junipers where it is protected from the ravages of man and other animals.

As the pastures rise towards the rocks, giving way to steep inclines littered with stones, the vegetation becomes more patchy but nonetheless endowed with many flowers. For here abounds the white-flowered Alpine poppy *(Papaver burseri)* and the Round-leaved pennycress *(Thlaspi rotundifolium)*, a dwarf crucifer with small, almost round, thick leaves and tiny, violet, rosy-pink or white flowers.

In other places there are many small mats of the broadleaved Mouse-ear chickweed *(Cerastium latifolium)* with its hairy, greyish leaves and white flowers which remind one a little of a flax flower. It is often surrounded by the Alpine toadflax *(Linaria alpina)* with its small, zygomorphic flowers of a matchless violet colour, contrasting with an orange patch which marks the centre of the corollas.

This type of locality is also the environment of

Some plants of the rocks and screes.
(Top left) Alpine poppy (Papaver burseri).
(Below left) Doronicum grandiflorum.
(Below) Alpine toadflax (Linaria alpina).
(Bottom) Androsace helvetica

64

A group of plants found in the pasturelands.
(Above) Armeria alpina.
(Above right) Trumpet gentian (Gentiana clusii).
(Centre right) Rubble dock (Rumex scutatus).
(Bottom right) Stemless carline thistle (Carlina acaulis)

an aromatic milfoil, *Achillea atrata*, the violet or blue Trumpet gentian *(Gentiana clusii)*, a rock jasmine, *Androsace helvetica*, with its cushions clinging to the rocks, and the scattered yellow flowers of two plants of the *Compositae, Doronicum grandiflorum* and *Leontodon montanum*.

Naturally the flora varies from one place to another, especially in those regions some distance apart. This variation enhances the native flora of the pastures which becomes characterized here and there by different species, such as the scented Black vanilla orchid *(Nigritella nigra)*, the Mt. Cenis bellflower *(Campanula cenisia)* and the Mt. Cenis violet *(Viola cenisia)* with its large, deep violet or lilac flowers.

Elsewhere we meet a small buttercup, *Ranunculus parnassifolium*, whose white flowers look like little porcelain cups on which the anthers stand out as a big splash of honey yellow, with its close relative the white Alpine buttercup *(Ranunculus alpestris)*.

Among the small stones which invade the grasses, we sometimes find one of the smallest phanerogams, the Chamois cress *(Hutchinsia alpina)*, with its crossed, four-petalled white flowers, or sometimes the large sulphur-yellow flowers of the Creeping avens *(Geum reptans)* which we have met elsewhere.

Other plants characterize pastures on siliceous soils composed of gneiss, crystalline schist and

(Above) Spring crocus (Crocus vernus) *which flourishes in the pasturelands immediately after the snow melts*

(Above right) Common columbine (Aquilegia vulgaris) *is one of the loveliest flowers to be found in the mountain grasslands*

granite. The flora is more varied and numerous in places which are scattered with rocks and stones, frequently matching the richness of the flora on the calcareous pastures.

We might find, for example, the Golden-flowered leopards-bane *(Doronicum clusii)*, often encroached upon by the modest, hairy Dwarf milfoil *(Achillea nana)*, or by the open, pink-purple corymbs of the white-leaved *Adenostyles leucophylla*. Between these flowers lie cushions of a rock jasmine, *Androsace vandelii*, a sister species to the calcicole *Androsace helvetica* which we have already mentioned.

The siliceous pastures support many species of the genus *Gentiana* such as the Stemless gentian *(Gentiana acaulis)* and the brilliant Spring gentian *(G. verna)*, as well as numerous pioneer species of the *Saxifragaceae*, like *Saxifraga biflora* with its white or rosy-pink flowers and the Purple saxifrage *(Saxifraga oppositifolia)* with its lilac-pink flowers. Both these saxifrage species have very small, tightly overlapping leaves around delicate stems.

Surely no visitor to the Alpine pastures can fail to notice, amongst the grasses, the silvery Stemless carline thistle *(Carlina acaulis)* with its great circular leaf-rosettes hugging closely to the ground. Despite the name of this species, there is a variety (var. *alpina*) which has a long stem during flowering. Another stemless thistle, common to the Alps in summer and autumn is the purple-headed *Cirsium acaulon* with its rosette of prickly, green leaves.

Among the less showy plants which are none-theless quite interesting are two knotweeds of the *Polygonaceae*, the very common Rubble dock *(Rumex scutatus)* with its helmet-shaped leaves and the rarer Mountain sorrel *(Oxyria digyna)* with its kidney-shaped leaves on long petioles, along with the Brownish woodrush *(Luzula alpinopilosa)*, the tiny Firm sedge *(Carex firma)*, the Dark sedge *(Carex atrata)* and *Poa alpina*, a grass with small violet-tinted spikes, which, at higher altitudes, gives the mountains an appearance like that of tundra. We also find some ferns like the Moon fern *(Botrychium lunaria)* and the Parsley fern *(Cryptogramma crispa)* which possess deeply divided, fertile fronds, different from the triangular sterile ones.

In fine weather after some rainfall, the alpine pastures can be covered with fruiting fungi. In particular we see the excellent, violet, *Tricholoma nudum*, some hygrophores, and the characteristic puff-balls which are very good to eat if cooked when they are very young. Two of the most common puff-ball species include *Lycoperdon gemmatum* with verrucose and furfuraceous fruiting bodies which can be as big as a walnut or even a little bigger, and *Lycoperdon giganteum* with fruiting bodies which can sometimes exceed the size of a man's head.

The tall herbs

Under 'tall herbs' we can deal with those plant communities which are found in the shady, cool and damp places. These communities usually consist of large or tall herbaceous plants. We have already come across many of these plants in the larchwood zone, and, to a greater extent, in the Green alder groves found in clearings where rich soil has accumulated in ground hollows, believed to have been created during the ice ages.

The distribution of this type of community, which we have called previously the 'megaphorbia', is linked with the other communities we have already described in which the species of the genera *Petasites*, *Carduus*, *Cirsium*, *Aconitum* and the taller species of *Gentiana* dominate. It looks most typical at the level of the alpine pastures where, if the dampness of the soil is favourable, a few of the various willow shrubs such as *Salix pentandra*, *Salix purpurea*, *Salix caesia*, and *Salix lapponum*, are joined, in the

The megaphorbia consists of tall, herbaceous plants. A common representative of the community is the Woolly thistle (Cirsium eriophorum)*, shown here*

barer patches, by the prickly thistles *Cirsium eriophorum* and *C. spinosissimum*. More common developments may be seen near the edges of alpine pastures and in ruderal areas, especially where there are manure pits (and hence soil which is rich in minerals) or against low, shady, dry-stone walls.

In the first case, at the edges of the alpine pastures, the Monk's rhubarb *(Rumex alpinus)* is a consistent inhabitant with its plumes of greenish-yellow flowers arising from patches of large basal leaves like those of the Good King Henry *(Chenopodium bonus-henricus)*, an insignificant weed belonging to the *Chenopodiaceae* whose leaves can be eaten like spinach.

Near the stone walls we find the Common nettle *(Urtica dioica)*, the Rose bay willowherb *(Epilobium angustifolium)* and the Burdock *(Arctium lappa)* which can sometimes grow at altitudes well over 1,500 m.

Tall herbs develop particularly along the banks of the brooks and rivers in the montane zone

River beds in flower

The waters which flow down from the glaciers melting in spring flow as narrow brooks and tiny cascades, and eventually join to form noisy torrents which incessantly polish the boulders lying in their path. This flow of water eventually slows down and deposits layers of slime onto the rocks, thus forming a suitable substratum, as the year draws by, for many kinds of plants.

If we study the Alpine river beds, we notice that the willow shrubs and the Green alder *(Alnus viridis)*, are joined by, and intermingled with, the Sea buckthorn *(Hippophae rhamnoides)*, a bushy shrub with ashen-grey, prickly branches and silvery leaves rather like those of the willows with which it lives. It is easily recog-

nized, however, by its unmistakeable, bright orange berries which are the size of garden peas, or perhaps a little smaller.

Another plant typical of the mountain river beds is *Myricaria germanica* which forms tall, glaucuous bushes, its branches covered with small, almost linear leaves, and with unobtrusive spikes of pink or white flowers.

Here and there the river bed becomes ablaze with purple due to the presence of two or more species of willowherbs: the often mentioned, showy Rose bay willowherb *(Epilobium angustifolium)*, which readily adapts to stony river beds and the more humble Alpine willowherb *(Epilobium fleischeri)* which is sometimes substituted by its close relative, *E. dodonaei*; both

Montane river beds are flooded during the spring melting of the snows and become covered with flowering plants as they dry out; in this photograph pink cushions of the Rock soapwort (Saponaria ocymoides) *can be seen*

these species are normally associated with muddy shingles and acid soils.

At altitudes of around 1,800 m to 2,000 m where the snow lingers long and the summer does not last long, the flood waters which come down from the glaciers cease after a relatively short period. Parts of these river beds, which can sometimes occupy very large areas, give way to the growth of dwarf shrubs and herbaceous plants which explode into colour from June to August. A surprising number of species grow so profusely in these river beds that they create the appearance of a carpet of flowers.

But each species, even in that flat, quiet, apparently homogenous environment adapts to its own most suitable 'micro-habitat'. And so, from the river banks, which run into the woods and shrublands, the sparse larches and the last few rhododendrons with their glowing flowers fade away and the Green alder becomes thicker, and eventually yields to the willowherbs and the monkshoods among the stones.

Towards the middle of the sandy, muddy river bed, islands of rich soil rise clear of the surrounding water, and here we find the plants which grow in the pastures gathered together; the early white and violet crocuses which soon vanish after spring, the Pyrenean buttercup *(Ranunculus pyrenaeus)*, the purple, Alpine clover *(Trifolium alpinum)*, the Golden rock-rose *(Helianthemum chamaecistus)* with its many varieties, the Long-spurred pansy *(Viola calcarata)*, the demure *Polygala alpestris* with its little blue-violet flowers, a cyclamen-coloured carnation, *Dianthus alpestre*, the soft cushions of the Rock soap-wort *(Saponaria ocymoides)* with its thousands of purple flowers, and the tight

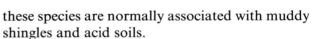

Some plants of the montane river beds. (Above) Colony of Dryas octopetala. *(Above left)* Epilobium fleischeri. *(Centre left)* Hippocrepis comosa. *(Below left)* Alsine laricifolia *in full bloom*

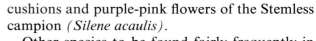

(Right) Pedicularis verticillata.
(Far right) Flower of Geum montanum.
(Below) Creeping avens (Geum reptans).
(Bottom left) Glacier buttercup (Ranunculus glacialis).
(Bottom right) Clumps of Saxifraga autumnalis *var.* aizoides *along a brook*

cushions and purple-pink flowers of the Stemless campion *(Silene acaulis).*

Other species to be found fairly frequently in these sporadic, grassy river beds include the Alpine blue flax *(Linum alpinum)*, the tiny, white Starry saxifrage *(Saxifraga stellaris)* and the Common kidney vetch *(Anthyllis vulneraria)*. Among the *Leguminosae* we can often meet the Mountain milk vetch *(Oxytropis jaquinius)* with its light blue flowers, the Meadow milk vetch *(Oxytropis campestris)* and the Horseshoe vetch *(Hippocrepis comosa)* which both have yellow corollas, as well as the showy, purple False vetch *(Astragalus monspessulanus)*. There are many examples from other families including the Whorled lousewort *(Pedicularis verticillata)* of the *Scrophulariaceae* with its lilac pink spikes, or other species

(Left) The Nivolet lakes in the Aosta Valley surrounded by pastures and scree slopes

(Below) Flowering Tanacetum alpinum, *a characteristic species in the high pastures*

related to it such as the simple Alpine bartsia *(Bartsia alpina),* and, from the *Gentianaceae,* the Spring gentian *(Gentiana verna),* with its intensely blue, star-shaped flowers.

In the less fertile places we see the broad sulphur-yellow flowers of the Creeping avens *(Geum reptans)* and the white, eight-petalled flowers of the Mountain avens *(Dryas octopetala).*

Near the cool streams, between cushions of the *Bryum* and *Philonotis* mosses, we see once again the Grass of Parnassus *(Parnassia palustris),* and the Yellow mountain saxifrage *(Saxifraga aizoides)* with its small, yellow, five-petalled flowers speckled with red. Often there are also beds of peat-moss (of the genus *Sphagnum*), and among them we can look to find two insectivorous plants which are difficult to see; the Common butterwort *(Pinguicula vulgaris)* with violet flowers, and the Alpine butterwort *(Pinguicula alpina)* with white blossoms.

It is not unusual, at around 2,000 m to 2,500 m altitude to find small, blue-green lakes with gently sloping, muddy banks. When the snows melt the waters here give new life to the prostrate bushes of a dwarf willow, *Salix herbacea,* and the marvellous Glacier buttercup *(Ranunculus glacialis)* with its delicate, white and pink honey-leaves.

The alpine tundra

Now we continue to climb higher, up beyond the flowering pastures, stopping before the bare rocks and the perennial snows to see the monotonous grassland communities. These are, in a certain sense, very similar to the types of vegetation found in the Arctic tundra and the Asian steppe; short grasslands occupied by only a few species, or, sometimes, by only one. They have an appearance like that of the Mat-grass growth which we have mentioned before and which is often common at these altitudes as well.

The main features of this vegetation are the dwarf sedges (*Carex* species). The Curved sedge (*Carex curvula*) grows to only 10 cm in height in a very close community which we call the *Curvuletum*. This occurs at altitudes between 2,500 m and 3,000 m, and is typical of the plateaux abandoned during glacial recession.

The *Curvuletum* has a typical ochrous colour because of a premature yellowing of the leaves. The plants are curved towards the base, hence their name, and they are rarely found in the company of other plants, apart, perhaps, from the viviparous form of the Alpina poa (*Poa alpina* var. *vivipara*) and *Polygonum viviparum*. Both these species, as their names indicate, form tiny bulbils in the spikes of their flowers and are thus able to reproduce asexually in an area where there are very few, if any, insects. Other grass species do occur but they are rare; for example, the Wild oat grass (*Arrhenatherum elatius*).

On calcareous soils two other sedge communities can develop: the secondary *Firmetum* and *Helinetum* often follow the pioneer vegetation which is based on the Mountain avens (*Dryas octopetala*) and dwarf willows such as *Salix herbacea* and *S. reticulata*.

The *Firmetum* is dominated by the thick growth of the sedge *Carex firma* on an understory of mosses and lichens. Its environment is normally dryish slopes, in terraces, from 2,000 m to almost 3,000 m altitude. The *Firmetum* is frequently brightened by red-pink speckled cushions of the Stemless campion (*Silene acaulis*) or by the white flowers of the Mountain avens (*Dryas octopetala*). Where it is not well developed, due to extreme environmental conditions such as the wind, dwarf willows or some saxifrages take root.

The *Helinetum* is characteristic of the calcareous soils with a less well developed humus layer, in places more exposed to the wind at around 3,000 m altitude which present almost prohibitive conditions to most other plants. It is recognizable by its discontinuity and by the rusty red colour of its turf which is formed by the dominant species, *Kobresia bellardii*, often accompanied by a tiny sedge with black spikes, the Dark sedge (*Carex atrata*), by gentians such as the Trumpet gentian (*Gentiana clusii*) and by a few members of the *Caryophyllaceae* family which can survive at these high altitudes.

Pasture and alpine tundra bordering a stream

Peat-bogs and snow-filled valleys

We have already mentioned some of the floristic components of the marshes that are often found around the conifer woodland and the pasturelands; marshes which contain in particular the Grass of Parnassus *(Parnassia palustris)*, tall sedges (*Carex* species), and the Meadowsweet *(Filipendula ulmaria)*.

We now turn to the peat-bogs, or those marshlands whose substratum is a spongy bed made by the presence of various peat mosses of the genera *Sphagnum* and *Polytrichum*, by other mosses, and by plants of the genera *Carex*, *Eriophorum*, *Juncus*, etc. which are adapted to waterlogged conditions. All these species were present throughout the Quaternary Period and have developed vast areas of peat. Water itself is not very much in evidence in the bogs, at least not on the surface. We only need to take a few steps onto the mire, however, and the bog immediately yields to the pressure to leave footprints which fill with water and become deeper and deeper as we go further from the edge.

We will disregard the bogs at lower altitudes and observe only those which we might find at altitudes between 1,500 m and 2,500 m. These are characterized by the presence of the peat mosses:

Sphagnum cymbifolium, S. acutifolium, S. amblyphyllum, S. subbicolor and hundreds of other species and varieties which are very difficult to recognize, even for specialists.

On top of this spongy mass, whose colour varies from a greenish-yellow ochre to grey-glaucous and from white to brown or purple, there grow mosses of the genera *Bryum, Philonotis, Polytrichum, Calliergon, Drepanocladus* and several others. Characteristic flowering plants which take root in the acid soil include various species of *Carex*, (e.g. *Carex fusca*), the cotton grasses, particularly *Eriophorum scheuchzeri* with its silvery, cotton-tufted heads, orchids like *Dactylorchis maculata,* the Grass of Parnassus *(Parnassia palustris)*, the Tormentil *(Potentilla erecta)*, a few sundews of the genus *Drosera*, the Alpine snowbell *(Soldanella alpina)* with its fringed lilac flowers rather like fringed skirts, and the smallest species of this genus, occuring in the eastern Alps, the pretty Least snowbell *(Soldanella minima)* with white flowers. We also find the violet-flowered Common butterwort *(Pinguicula vulgaris)* and its white-flowered relative, the Alpine butterwort *(Pinguicula alpina)*.

Here and there the peat-bogs preserve rare

View of a peat-bog high in the Aosta Valley

(Right) Marsh at a high altitude. The Cotton grass (Eriophorum scheuchzeri) *is in full bloom*

Two typical flowers of the wet places in high mountains. (Right) Alpine snowbell (Soldanella alpina). *(Far right) Alpine butterwort* (Pinguicula alpina)

floral relics of the ice ages, such as a cranberry, *Vaccinium oxycoccus*, with its red berries, and the Marsh andromeda *(Andromeda polifolia)*, a rare ericaceous shrub which grows only a little more than 10 cm high.

Now we should go higher, beyond the alpine tundra to the foot of the glaciers. Here we find the snow-filled valleys, a severe and selective environment at altitudes from 2,500 m to 3,500 m, whose substratum varies from a thin slime to a rocky rubble which is rich in minerals and constantly very damp. The growing season is extremely short in these habitats; it is reduced to only one or two months and comes after the spring snows have melted.

It is obvious that in such an environment the flora is limited to a few species. Regular inhabitants include a few lichens *(Cetraria islandica, C. nivalis,* and *Stereocaulon alpinum)*, some mosses *(Polytrichum sexangulare* and *Rhacomitrium canescens)*, a few sedges *(Carex foetida, C. curvula* and *C. nigra)*, and, above all, a prostrate and twisted dwarf willow, *Salix herbacea,* which grows only a few centimetres above the ground, and is capable of surviving in almost all localities, withstanding frost and wind, the water from the snows and the dazzling light of the sun at altitudes of 3,000 m. But when the snows melt prematurely and recede quickly the snow-filled valleys become bedecked with flowers. Once again we see the Glacier buttercup *(Ranunculus glacialis)*, the Alpine marguerite *(Tanacetum alpinum)* often represented by a small variety (var. *minimum*) bearing a single white flower which is almost flush with the ground, and frequently accompanied by its close relative *Leucanthemum atratum* with its flowers enveloped by black scales.

75

Towards the peaks

We have now reached the heights where even such words as grandeur and majesty seem insufficient. It is not hard, as one looks out over the green valleys towards the peaks, to understand the dedication of the mountaineer and his sense of achievement.

The greatest impressions at these altitudes are perhaps those of the boldness of nature, and the immensity of the forces which raised these giant structures to their great heights. We also notice, of course, the constant workings of many natural agencies changing and moulding the shapes we see outlined against the sky: the wind and rain, running water, the temperature variations between sharp frosts and the heat of the day, and, most of all, the vast glaciers.

The effects of this erosion are often very dramatic. We might see enormous natural amphitheatres where it seems that the words of the Greek dramatists should be heard over the moaning of the wind. Giant crags take on extraordinary shapes, silhouetted against an evening sky, and ravines appear at our feet, plunging vast distances into semi-darkness. The moraines left by the inexorable workings of great glaciers punctuate the wastelands of sheer rock.

It might at first be thought that these areas are as barren and desolate as they are awesome, but we find that there is a surprisingly diverse flora still able to survive. This is not always immediately apparent because the vegetation is restricted to very small plants and is sparse everywhere.

We can now pass on to examine the part of this vegetation persisting on the crags which emerge from the glaciers at altitudes from about 2,700 m to well over 3,000 m. We can also look at the meagre flora which pioneers the rocky wastes and the small moraines which are isolated on all sides from the surrounding rocks by glaciers.

Among the plants which flourish most at this altitude we find lichens (particularly *Stereocaulon alpinum*), mosses (e.g. *Rhacomitrium canescens*) a few grasses (e.g. *Agrostis rupestris*) and sedges (e.g. *Carex microstyla*). In particular we find several flowering dicotyledons: *Arabis serpyllifolia*, *Sisymbrium dentatum*, *Cerastium alpinum*, *Silene acaulis*, *Sedum alpestre*, *Potentilla sibbaldi*, *Androsace alpina*, *Veronica alpina*, *Senecio incanus*, and *Linaria alpina*, usually accompanied by the grey, hairy *Gnaphalium supinum* and the Glacier buttercup *(Ranunculus glacialis)* which we have already come across in the snow-filled valleys.

We can now observe a sloping moraine beneath the walls of rock which consists of a chaotic heap of stony debris, covered with patches of the black and yellow thalli of lichens. Despite the obvious mobility of this eroding substratum it can still harbour a rare flora.

Once again we find the dwarf Herbaceous willow *(Salix herbacea)*, along with the wonderful Creeping azalea *(Loiseleuria procumbens)* with its bright purple flowers, the eight-petalled Mountain avens *(Dryas octopetala)* and *Linaria alpina* pioneering this shifting habitat. Sometimes they are joined by the delicate, dwarf King of the Alps *(Eritrichum nanum)* with its sky-blue flowers; this plant can quite frequently be found in between the cracks in the steepest rocks, within sight of the eagles, together with *Petrocallis pyrenaica* with its yellow, crossed flowers.

A very rare moss, *Voitia nivalis*, appears almost to follow the paths of the wild goats and the chamois since it can only be found where they stay for some time and deposit their excrement.

The mountain walls and the high rocks, fissured and worn by frost and wind over the ages, harbour several flowers of a rare beauty which creep onto the rocks and are often associated with clumps of the Alpine bent grass *(Agrostis rupestris)*.

These rocks are invariably covered with the yellow lichens *(Rhizocarpon geographicum* and *R. calcareum)*, the red ones *(Caloplaca callopisma* and *C. elegans)* and the grey ones (especially of the genera *Verrucaria*, *Aspicilia* and *Gyrophora*). These lichens are often accompanied by black mosses of the genera *Grimmia*, *Andreaea*, *Dicranoweisia* and *Distichium*.

It is possible in these regions, as it is in the

A huge natural amphitheatre of rocks high in the mountains

alpine pasturelands, to draw a distinction between the flora of the calcareous and dolomitic rocks and the flora of the granitic or basic rocks.

The first type includes the beautiful, densely crowded hummocks of a rock jasmine, *Androsace helvetica* with its pink flowers, frequently accompanied by the glaucous ones of *Saxifraga caesia* with its white flowers and *Saxifraga mutata* with its orange flowers.

Elsewhere appears a hairy umbellifer, *Athamantha cretensis*, with its filiform, laciniate leaves; a plant which often grows no higher than 8–10 cm. We also find the miniscule Mt. Cenis bellflower (*Campanula cenisia*), *Cerastium latifolium* with its hairy, ash-grey leaves and wide, white flowers, *Achillea atrata*, the dwarf *Arabis pumila*, *Draba tomentosa*, and the Rock valerian (*Valeriana saxatilis*).

The granitic rocks also play host to a rock jasmine though it is a different species, *Androsace vandelii*. On these rocks we find too the cushion colonies of the Mountain houseleek (*Sempervivum montanum*) or the Cobweb houseleek (*Sempervivum arachnoideum*) with its cobweb-like mats of hairs, the tiny Least primrose (*Primu-*

la minima) with its purple flowers peeping out of a rosette of basal leaves, the aromatic, sought after *Artemisia genipi* and *Artemisia laxa*, and a number of saxifrages (*Saxifraga moschata*, *S. adpera* and *S. exarata*).

Naturally, the flora of the highest peaks is affected not only by the different types of substrata but also by the degree of exposure and the conséquent variation in the duration of light and the ranges of temperature and humidity. Indeed, we should recall that we observed in the woodlands on northern, exposed areas tree trunks which were covered in mosses and lichens. So, too, at this high altitude, the rocks which show their face to the sun become dotted with small grasses and flowering plants. The side of the rocks in the shade has at the most a very poor flora, often limited to microscopic, epiphytic algae which appear to stain them with dark green and black brush strokes.

If we continue to climb, the question of course arises: are there any further plants to find? It is well known that in the Himalayas and the Andean grasslands, herbaceous plants can survive even beyond 5,000 m altitude. In the Alps the thalli of

Four species found on the high Alpine rocks. (Top left) Galium pusillum. (Top right) Senecio incanus subsp. carniolicus. (Bottom left) Artemisia glacialis var. mutellina. (Bottom right) Artemisia glacialis

the lovely red-lead coloured lichen *Caloplaca elegans* are often present, demonstrating a remarkable range in altitude from the stone roofs of the lowland Alpine huts to the otherwise almost naked rocks at well over 6,600 m altitude.

Various authors quote about a dozen plants which are present above 4,000 m altitude in the Alps and they provide a list. In this book we will just quote the names of species to be found on the Matterhorn in Switzerland: *Phyteuma pedamontanum* ascends to 4,010 m altitude; *Androsace alpina, Gentiana brachyphylla, Poa alpina* var. *minor, Saxifraga aspera* var. *bryoides, Saxifraga biflora* and *Saxifraga muscoides*, all ascend to 4,200 m altitude. As can be seen the saxifrages are the plants which are most numerous.

The maximum altitude at which a flowering plant has been found in Europe is 4,272 m. The Glacier buttercup (*Ranunculus glacialis*) was found at this height on the rocks of the Finster-aarhorn in Switzerland.

The mosses can, of course, grow higher up in the Alpine range, and some species of *Grimmia* have been collected at altitudes of 4,559 m and 4,638 m on Mount Rosa. On the same mountain and at similar altitudes lichen species of the genera *Cetraria, Parmelia, Gyrophora, Rhizocarpon,* and *Lecanora* have also been found.

Up to these altitudes, plant life has always been visible; we now know, however, that both at those altitudes quoted and above them, there are numerous microscopic planktonic algae belonging to the *Diatomeae* and the *Chloroficeae* living on the snowfields and the glaciers. It is to the algae that we can attribute the so-called 'red-snow' which occurs on several mountain systems and on the polar ice-fields and which has always impressed naturalists and explorers.

From the Rockies to the Andes

A glance at the map will tell us that geographically the more important mountain ranges of the American continent have a north-south orientation. They reach, from the Arctic region, vast distances through the Equator and almost to the Antarctic regions. This means, of course, that the floristic distribution along these ranges is governed as much by the latitude as by altitude.

In Alaska, the predominant vegetation is tundra, with many mosses, lichens and conifer forests, except for the highest, perennially snow-clad peaks where there is a flourishing alpine flora. The vast range of the Rocky Mountains begins at latitude 65°N. and traverses an entire continent down to 30°N. at which point it joins, practically without a break, the Mexican Sierras which then continue right down past the Tropic of Cancer. It

is natural, therefore to find considerable variation in the succession of vegetation types, and we can see this, for example, in the conifer forests of the Rocky Mountains. On the eastern slopes we notice the Oregon pines and the firs, while on the western slopes we see the Tuja and Sequoia forests near the Pacific. The mountains eventually pass to the immense prairies or mountain deserts of which the ones in Colorado and Arizona are the most classic examples. These grasslands are rich in succulent *Cactaceae* and there are thousands of sage bushes and herbaceous plants with brilliantly and diversely coloured, but short-lived, flowers.

Returning to the Rocky Mountains themselves, we recall that they have many communities which are fairly reminiscent, at least physiognomically

Mountain avens (Dryas octopetala) *is widely distributed, both in the Alps and the tundra*

(Above) View of the tundra among the mountains of Alaska

of those in the European mountain chains, with great forests of birch and elm whose undergrowth has a profusion of rhododendrons and whortle-berries as well as exotic plants like the Poison ivy (*Rhus toxicendron*).

On the mountains of the most northern tropical regions of the New World there is a basal zone of woodlands which are continuous with those of the surrounding plain. Then, as the mountain slopes are ascended, we come to the *Podocarpus* forests, belonging to a genus of conifers peculiar to these territories. Further up the mountain, as we have seen in the European Alps, the arboreal vegetation gradually thins out and finally ceases. Higher up still, where the climate is much colder and drier, the great expanses of the Andean alpine vegetation called the 'Paramos' stretch as far as the eye can see. This vegetation is extremely sparse, consisting almost entirely of prostrate

woody plants and tall grasses (especially of the genera *Calamagrostis* and *Deschampsia*), mixed with a number of showy *Compositae* of the genera *Culcitium* and *Espeletia*. Elsewhere, however, in other South American alpine reaches, the grass-land stretches consist predominantly of cushion-forming clumps of *Festuca*.

On the mountains of Mexico the tropical climatic conditions cause special modifications to the vegetation, though the lower slopes are often covered with temperate-like forests that possess very few tropical characteristics. Above altitudes from 3,000 m to 3,500 m snow can fall in this part of the world throughout the year although in the summer it normally melts immediately, persisting only briefly at altitudes below 4,000 m. The level around 4,600 m altitude can be estab-lished as the lower limit of the perennial snows on these mountains whose peaks are often above

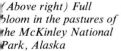
(Above right) Full bloom in the pastures of the McKinley National Park, Alaska

5,000 m. Frosts occur practically every night at these altitudes.

If we climb, then, from the humid tropical forest of the basal regions to roughly around 700 m altitude we find the oak woods which, in turn, give way to enormous conifer woods at around 1,800 m. The distribution of the conifers continues further south from Mexico to Guatemala and beyond. They consist of many species of pines and firs which often reach very imposing sizes.

An altitudinal division of the vegetation, according to Eyre (see the reading list on page 128), occurs between 2,000 m and 3,000 m at the so-called lower pine zone, mainly characterized at this level by pure woods of *Pinus montezumae*, although this tree may sometimes be accompanied by oaks and cedars.

Higher up, from 3,000 m to 3,500 m altitude, in a region of heavy rainfall, we find the fir zone with forests of *Abies religiosa*, sometimes mixed with broadleaved deciduous and evergreen trees and rich in a bushy undergrowth. Then, between 3,500 m and 4,000 m the pine and juniper forest characterized by *Pinus hartwegii* and *Juniperus tetragona* form the so-called upper pine belt, where the undergrowth is rich in tall grasses. From the branches of the conifers hang long beards of lichens of the genus *Usnea*, very similar to the 'wood beard' of the montane conifers in the European Alps.

Above the limit of the pine forests comes the alpine zone, with grasslands of many *Gramineae* of the genera *Festuca*, *Calamagrostis*, *Aira* and *Sporobolus*, together with many other flowering plants such as lupins (e.g. *Lupinus montanus*), thistle-like eryngos (e.g. *Eryngium protaeforum*) and many species of the *Cruciferae*.

These herbaceous formations sometimes rise to

Helianthella uniflora
in full bloom in the
Grand Teton National
Park, Wyoming

an altitude of 4,400 m or more and eventually give way to the glaciers and high-alpine rocks where only a few rare, isolated, herbaceous plants, as well as mosses and lichens, survive.

The Mexican Sierras are linked with the Cordilleras of Colombia and Venezuela, having a poor, tropical montane vegetation of a steppe or desert-like nature. This vegetation is similar to that which occupies part of the temperate grasslands on the alpine zones of the Andes Cordillera between the Equator and Patagonia.

The Andes themselves tower up from the still partly virgin tropical rain forests called the 'Selvas', from the Gran Chaco to the east with its rose-wood, cedars and balsa trees, and from the steppe-like or desert zones to the west. On these mountains there are huge stretches of the 'Paramos' and 'Puna' vegetation. 'Puna' vegetation is a sparse, thorny scrub found on dry plateaux which is only suitable, in economic terms, for rough pasture. Beyond the 'Puna' (in an altitudinal sense) are 'islands' of really high-alpine flora.

Let us now consider each zone of the Andes in turn, working upwards from the foothill forests to the high-alpine flora.

At this point we must mention that in Colombia, as in other woodland zones, the forests flourish up to about 1,200 m altitude or a little beyond, and include, amongst many other plants, several tropical lowland trees such as palms which give way, in slightly more temperate forest areas to arboreal ferns and thickets of bamboo.

This luxuriant and humid Colombian forest changes on the Andes to cool, damp, mossy, thickly wooded, often marshy and foggy forest which, on both slopes of the Cordillera, can rise to between 3,500 m and 4,000 m altitude. This is collectively known as the Elfin woodland, or,

(Above) Forest of conifers and broadleaved trees at the foot of the mountains along Lake Teslin, in the Yukon

84

(Right) Example of the more or less monotypic flora which grows at an altitude of about 4,300 m in Venezuela; the illustrated species is Espeletia grandiflora

(Right) Cacti of considerable size mingle with the herbaceous scrub vegetation near Camargo in Upper Bolivia

locally, as 'ceja de la montana', and it consists of a single layer of small, contorted trees, 5–10 m tall, belonging to the genera *Polyepis* and *Myrica*. The humid climate allows mosses, ferns and lycopods to grow between the trees, many of which are epiphytes on the branches. Unfortunately, man has exploited this vegetation for a long time so that now vast tracts of degraded woodland have been transformed into the 'matorral' scrub which includes *Baccharis* bushes and plants related to the cultivated fuchsias of the genus *Gynoxis*.

Let us now climb to the 'Paramos' or 'Pajonales', the terms used locally in the northern Andes to describe the great, treeless, scrubby lands, of the alpine zone. These vast, cold lands extend from 3,300 m to about 4,300 m altitude.

The flora has an abundance of tall grasses of the genera *Stipa*, *Calamagrostis* and *Festuca* with an intermingling of several other flowering, herbaceous plants such as *Achyrophorus quitensis* and *Gentiana diffusa*.

From altitudes of about 4,000 m upwards the flora becomes relatively unvaried, though rich in quantity. The plants here do not occupy the ground uniformly but form sporadic, dense colonies; the gaps between them are often filled with residual snow. Above 4,600 m it snows frequently and the flowering plants become rare.

High up in the western Andes and in the eastern Andes of Bolivia, we find the dry, open 'Puna', a desert steppe which is composed mainly of plants from the *Gramineae* (of the genera *Stipa* and *Festuca*) and of woody shrubs of the *Compositae*. This dwarf shrub zone provides the meagre pasture for the large South American mammals such as the lama, the vicuna and the alpaca. Other associated plants include species of the genera *Culcitium*, *Polylepis*, *Pourretia*, *Lupinus*, *Trichocereus*, *Opuntia*, and *Azorella*. In some cases the 'Puna' becomes even poorer, more arid, and drought-ridden and it then takes the local name of 'Tola'.

The vegetation of high Peru takes on a special appearance where the cacti and shrubs abound. Cactaceous examples include *Cereus peruvianus* and *C. sepium* with their small white flowers; above 4,000 m altitude, we find *Loghocereus macrostibas* growing to 4–5 m in height amid a carpet of stemless herbaceous plants.

(Left) A very fine example of Puja raimondii *at about 3,800 m altitude in southern Peru*

(Right) Sporadic pampas vegetation near Lake Viedma on the Cordillera in Patagonia

The mountains of Asia

As in the American continents, the vast territory of Asia is affected by a very wide range of differing climates. These climates pass from the extreme continental climates of the centre, where the land is occupied largely by steppes and deserts, to the oceanic climates of the Far East, and from the very cold climates of the Arctic belt to the equatorial climates of southern India, Ceylon, Malaya and the large islands of Indonesia. Naturally all these climatic zones have a characteristic vegetation.

On the whole, the regions around the Arctic Circle and above 60°N. are occupied by immense conifer forests of firs, larches, and pines called the 'taiga'. This extends from Scandinavia practically as far as the Far East. As one goes northwards, the wood-tundra of pines and birches gradually becomes the scrub and herbaceous tundra. Going southward we reach the mixed, deciduous forests, which then fragment into very different vegetation zones because of the warmer and more humid climate. In the central Asian region we see the establishment of the mixed equatorial forests which, with the increase of altitude, culminates in the mountain flora of the Himalayan massif.

(Right) Extraordinary terracing for rice cultivation on a steep slope at about 1,800 m altitude; southern Himalayan mountains, Nepal

(Below left) Montane woodland at 1,800 m altitude; Nepal

(Below) Conifer forest at about 1,600 m altitude; near Charikot, Nepal

The flora in the mountains of northern Asia does not differ much in appearance from that of the mountains of northern Europe and there are quite a number of alpine species common to all the sub-Arctic ranges of the Eurasian continent, just as other zones in Asia, such as the conifer forests of the 'taiga', are related to those in Europe.

The vegetation types found in the Himalayan complex are more differentiated than those of the European Alps. On the southern slopes the foothill vegetation imperceptibly mixes with the tropical rainforest.

Higher up, at around 2,500 m altitude, the slopes are clad by mixed, deciduous broadleaved trees, especially species of *Quercus* and *Aesculus*, related to the European oaks and horse-chestnuts. These woodlands are succeeded, as we climb, by woodlands of needle-leaved conifers (of the genera *Pinus*, *Picea*, *Abies* and *Cedrus*).

The series of zones which follows has a similar pattern to that found on the European Alps. The woodlands are followed by small, shrubby plants (up to a couple of metres tall) but those in the Himalayas usually have even more brilliantly coloured flowers. Examples include many species of rhododendrons and azaleas which are often cultivated in Europe for ornamental purposes.

Around altitudes between 3,400 m and 4,000 m there is still a great deal of shrub vegetation with many beautiful rhododendrons and willows in addition to the dazzling herb flora which is composed of species of many genera such as *Leontopodium*, *Gentiana*, *Ranunculus*, and *Saussurea*, to name but a few.

The southern slopes of the Himalayan chain are rather humid and rich in mountain streams because of condensation from the warm, damp air currents which rise from the Indian Ocean. The northern slopes, however, are much colder and drier, because they are swept for long periods of the year by the cold, dry winds which howl down over the inhospitable deserts of Mongolia.

On these northern slopes the vegetation is mainly steppic in origin although the grassy carpet is rarely well developed. The flora becomes very sporadic at high altitudes, and consists mainly of species of the *Gramineae* from the genera *Stipa*, *Festuca* and *Avena*, *Cyperaceae* from the genus *Carex*, *Compositae* of the genus *Taraxacum* as well as many species of the genera *Ranunculus* and *Primula*.

As on the Alps, after climbing still higher we find that the herbaceous vegetation becomes very sparse though still maintaining a steppic appearance. Eventually, however, we see vast areas of arid, open ground, scattered only here and there

with tufts of grasses between the boulders and rocks, and these grow right up to the snowline.

A few saxifrages and mosses take root in cracks and cavities, pushing their way through patches of lichens, and survive on the rock faces which sometimes protrude out of the snowfields. Even these plants fail to keep their hold, however, if the rock face is completely exposed to the dry, northerly winds which can be very violent.

Let us now briefly examine the mountain chains of south-western Asia, in that vast zone which extends from Iran and Afghanistan to the Caucasus and Asia Minor, through to the shores of the Mediterranean.

It is easy to guess that these arid lands are largely steppe-like regions inhabited by tamarisks (of the genus *Tamarix*), large members of the *Umbelliferae*, many, often prickly members of the *Leguminosae*, (particularly species of the genus *Astragalus*) and members of the *Compositae*

(Above) Conifers on the mountains of Kashmir at 2,400 m altitude

(Right) A characteristic member of the Compositae *found in the Himalayas; the Everlasting pearl* (Anaphalis triplinervis)

90

such as the sagebrushes (of the genus *Artemisia*). This flora has many affinities with that on the mountains of the Mediterranean basin on both the European and the African shores, from the Middle East to the Iberian peninsular.

In fact it is possible to distinguish a basal plain consisting of the Aleppo pine *(Pinus halepensis)*, the Cork-oak *(Quercus suber)*, the Holm oak *(Q. ilex)* and the Turkey oak *(Q. cerris)*, often with formations of stunted Mediterranean maquis in which we find the Strawberry tree *(Arbutus unedo)*, the Turpentine tree *(Pistacia lentiscus)*, the Oleaster *(Olea oleaster)*, the Broadleaved phyllary *(Phyllirea latifolia)*, and the Tree erica *(Erica arborea)*.

Higher up, we find stretches of a sub-Mediterranean belt of mixed deciduous broadleaved trees including the Sweet chestnut *(Castanea sativa)*, the Manna ash *(Fraxinus ornus)*, the Field maple *(Acer campestre)*, the Black hornbeam *(Ostrya carpinifolia)* and the Beech *(Fagus silvatica)* which can appear in the cooler valleys. Eventually, these broadleaved trees are succeeded at higher altitudes by the fir forests. In the alpine zone, we see dwarf shrubs (especially *Juniperus communis)*, and grasslands with *Gramineae* (from the genera *Festuca, Sesleria* and *Nardus)*. This zone is followed by the belt of sporadic vegetation on the high rocks which is quite often rich in small flowering plants. These sprout from the crevices in the rocks and from the unstable scree slopes. Predominant species belong to the same genera as those found on the European Alps and include, amongst others, poppies and the dwarf willows.

The flora of the mountains of tropical and south-eastern Asia including large islands of Indonesia such as Sumatra and Java is very different from that of Central Asia. Here, in the equatorial rainforests, we find many very beautiful species such as the magnolias, casuarinas and podocarps which gird the mountain foothills and sometimes climb a little way up the slopes. But then, from about 1,000 m or 1,500 m up to 2,200 m, in cold, humid and windy conditions, they are replaced by the mossy evergreen forests, dominated by species of *Quercus*. These forests contain a number of deciduous trees and also include large numbers of stunted conifers which are quite different to the conifer forests at higher altitudes. The humid climate allows considerable epiphytic development, but the ferns and epiphytic orchids of the warmer tropical rainforests are substituted here by mosses and lichens.

The mountain forest becomes sparser and eventually gives way to a few contorted evergreens such as laurel and conifers in much the same way that we have seen, on the lower slopes of the European Alps, chestnut and beechwoods give way to the dwarf pines.

Around 2,400 m or a little higher, the arboreal vegetation gradually thins out until it is replaced by an alpine zone of shrubs and grassland. The shrubs belong to a number of familiar mountain genera such as *Vaccinium* and *Rhododendron* and to native genera such as *Ardisia*. As the shrub vegetation gets shorter and more prostrate, with more contorted branches, they leave wide spaces occupied solely by herbaceous plants of a very similar nature to those found on the mountains of the northern, more temperate areas.

Higher up still, we find a typical alpine vegetation which includes many endemic species like the Javan edelweiss *(Anaphalis javanica)* and others from the genera *Gentiana, Potentilla, Primula, Ranunculus, Euphrasia* and *Valeriana*.

(Above left) Tibetan gentian (Gentiana thibetica)

(Above) A gentian common in the Alps (of the Gentiana acaulis *group) which is also found in the Himalayas; the illustration shows a colony growing at an altitude of 3,530 m in Nepal*

The mountains of tropical Africa

Let us consider, in a brief panorama, the alpine flora of the mountain ranges of tropical Africa, those in Ethiopia and those of equatorial Africa proper; in particular, Kenya, Ruwenzori (Uganda) and Kilimanjaro (Tanzania). We can then examine separately the mountains of Cameroun and Madagascar.

Without wishing to make any specific distinctions we can say without doubt that the most unusual and interesting alpine plants of the East African mountains are the arborescent, thick-stemmed senecios *(Senecio* species of the family *Compositae)*, and lobelias *(Lobelia* species belonging to the family *Campanulaceae)* which have widespread herbaceous relatives of a much smaller size in many other regions of the world. There are about twenty species of tropical alpine senecios and lobelias and each one is distributed on a particular mountain or in a narrow area and is isolated from its close relatives by vast tracts of lowland tropical rainforest. Both the lobelias and the senecios to which we refer have a tall, thick, woody stem bearing multiple rosettes of leaves which terminate in large, cylindrical spikes of flowers.

Two of the most spectacular examples from these genera are *Senecio keniodendron* which is found in the tablelands of Kenya and reaches a height of 7 m, and *Lobelia rhyncopetala.*

The most spectacular lobelias are to be found in the high Semien of Uganda at altitudes between 3,600 m and 4,400 m. Both species occupy the open, Afro-alpine zone of grasslands where the predominant vegetation consists of sedges from the genus *Carex* (such as *C. monostachya*). These sedges produce large, wig-like cushions which are formed by clusters of long, curved, linear leaves falling around the flowering stems.

The mountain foothill vegetation of tropical Africa is similar to the foothill vegetation of tropical Asia in that it is merely an extension of the surrounding vegetation. The lowland northern slopes of Mount Kilimanjaro, for example, are enveloped by tropical savanna, while the southern slopes are covered by tropical rain-forest; a similar rainforest girds the western slopes of the Ruwenzori lowlands.

If we now work upwards, from the foothills, through each successive vegetation zone, we find that the second zone is composed of a more transitional, temperate type of rainforest; this is followed by damp, mossy forests, colonized by species of the genus *Podocarpus*, extensive colonies of *Juniperus procera*, a profusion of other shrub species from other genera, lianas and many epiphytic plants including orchids, ferns, mosses and lichens. The zone immediately above the mossy forests, particularly those on Ruwenzori and Kilimanjaro, is occupied by extensive stretches of bamboo. Above this we find a zone of arborescent *Erica* heath and this is followed by the alpine scrub and grassland containing the giant lobelias and senecios.

This alpine zone peters out into the poorer grasslands and peat-bogs which are continually washed by torrential rains and melt-waters from the snowfields further up. The snow line itself oscillates around an altitude of 5,000 m and here the vegetation becomes entirely herbaceous. Principal plants include species of the *Gramineae* (of the genus *Poa*), *Juncaceae* (of the genus *Luzula*) and small *Cruciferae* (of the genus *Arabis*). On the whole it is almost the same kind of vegetation which characterizes the high-alpine pasturelands and the sporadic turf zone of the European Alps.

It may now be useful to give some details about the distribution of some of the more important species and vegetation types found on the Cameroun mountains of West Africa. There are no giant senecios here, but there are several lobelias. Among the less showy plants which are also to be found here are some endemic species of the everlasting or straw-flowers *(Helichrysum* species), the lady's mantles *(Alchemilla* species*)*, the sowthistles *(Sonchus* species*)* as well as *Echinops* species, and numerous examples from the *Gentianaceae, Primulaceae,* and *Ericaceae.* At an altitude of about 1,800 m we meet a lovely arborescent fern, *Alsophila camerunensis,* and still higher up, at roughly 3,000 m the woody

(Right) Arborescent senecios at 4,000 m altitude in the Ruwenzori mountains, East Africa

(Left) Magnificent specimen of Cupressus duprezzyana at an altitude of 1,800 m in the Tassili N'Ajjer mountains, Algerian Sahara

vegetation disappears and grasslands prevail. This grassy zone is followed, at 3,500 m, by a spectacular alpine vegetation including beautiful endemics of the genera *Clematis, Viola, Geranium* and of the family *Dipsacaceae*.

A word now about the mountains of Madagascar. The foothills are surrounded, up to an altitude of about 800 m, by the tropical rainforest. At an altitude of less than 2,000 m the vegetation has completely passed to a montane forest rich in epiphytic lichens which hang from the boughs of the trees and become the major characteristic of this zone. At higher altitudes we come to the upper montane scrub vegetation with evergreen shrubs related to the laurels and heather. There is no true alpine development vegetation and the *Erica* heath grows right up to

the summit of the mountains.

In the arid, stony, rocky areas in the mountain chains of tropical Africa, we frequently come across succulent plants and other sclerophyllous xerophytes like the ones we noticed in the mountain deserts or prairies of America. These include the cactus-like stem succulents of the genus *Euphorbia*, species of the genera *Haworthia* (of the family *Liliaceae*) and *Caralluma* in Southern Rhodesia, and carrion flowers of the genera *Stapelia* and *Heurnia*, such as *Stapelia nobilis* of the mountains near the coast of the Somali Republic and *Heurnia bicampanulata* of the Transvaal. The carrion flowers are notorious plants because of their large, bizarre flowers which give off a nauseating smell like dead meat to attract large blowflies which pollinate them.

Alpine plants in cooking and medicine

Besides using the leaves, fruit and edible seeds for consumption, ancient man must have understood those parts of the plants which in some way could be useful to him in alleviating his ills and healing his wounds. We now know, in fact, how very rich the plant kingdom is in pharmaceutical chemicals.

It is not possible to set a clear dividing line between those plants which provide perfumed and aromatic substances and those which have medicinal properties. Nor is it possible to draw a firm distinction between the latter plants and those whose leaves and fruit are lethally poisonous, since, in both cases, it is often a question of establishing the most useful or pernicious dose which is, in turn, often dependent upon the susceptibilities and sensitivities of the individual.

We must, of course, decide on the order to follow in this brief review of aromatic, medicinal and poisonous alpine plants. The systematic order is, of course, the most natural and scientific one, but to follow this would mean that we must examine identical parts of widely different plants which would lead us to repeat, over and over again, very similar uses. It would therefore be better to choose a more elementary, familiar method and merely to describe the utilization of individual plants or their parts.

Let us begin, for instance, with the various wild species of garlic whose culinary use is so famous. These species are quite common; they are found in habitats ranging from dry, sunny places, to wet, cool woods. In the sunny places, on the rocks and in the meadows, we find the Wild chive *(Allium schoenoprasum)* with its almost globose, pink-lilac inflorescences and its small bulbs grouped into bunches. Both the bulbs and the leaves give food a pleasant, piquant and aromatic flavour and it is a plant which is, of course, often cultivated.

According to some authorities, a second species, the Ramsons *(Allium ursinum)* which is found in shady places and has a small umbellate inflorescence of white flowers, is also very useful

(Below left) Small bush of Wild thyme (Thymus serpyllum) *one of the best aromatic plants in the mountain flora*

(Below) The Cranberry (Vaccinium vitis-idaea); *its fruit is like that of the bilberry and can be eaten fresh or used in preserves*

Spotted Gentian (Gentiana punctata) *in blossom. Its rhizomes can be used in the same way as those of the related Great yellow gentian* (Gentiana lutea); *when properly administered as a tincture or an infusion they have a eupeptic action*

in the kitchen. It should be picked when young and is used mainly to season butter and cheeses. It also has tonic and purgative properties and locals use it to treat high blood-pressure.

One of the most important families, with a profusion of aromatic and medicinal plants, is certainly the *Labiatae*. Most of our familiar herbs belong to this family, including Sage, Rosemary, Marjoram, Balm, Hyssop and Old English lavender *(Lavandula spica)*. Old English lavender forms great bushes on the most sunny slopes of European mountains and it is not only gathered but also cultivated for distillation because of its excellent perfume. Domestically, from ancient times right up to the present day, its flowers have been used to perfume household linen.

Wild thyme *(Thymus serpyllum)* also belongs to the *Labiatae*. With its clusters of pink-lilac flowers, we see it at the submontane levels and right up to the high pastures where it becomes more intensely coloured and aromatic. Its leaves

are an excellent flavouring agent, rich in essential oils such as thymol which serve as an expectorant infusion, a carminative and as an aid to digestion.

Also belonging to the same family is Origanum *(Origanum vulgare)*, a more noticeable plant than Wild thyme, due to its more ovate leaves and larger inflorescences; we often see Origanum along mule-tracks and hedges, and in very exposed places.

When the leaves and stems of Origanum are dried out and reduced to powder or ground into small pieces it makes an excellent seasoning for salads and sauces. As an infusion it can be used as a carminative and eupeptic; in the form of a boiled tea it is excellent for the treatment of diarrhoea, and, as a gargle, for pharingitis and soreness of the gums.

The mints (species of the genus *Mentha*) whose aromatic and flavouring powers are universally well-known, are also members of the *Labiatae*.

The *Umbelliferae* is another family which contains many useful and richly aromatic plants; Parsley, Celery and Fennel are commonly cultivated edible examples. Many other species of this family can be found in the mountains, such as the Caraway *(Carum carvi)* and Cumin *(Cuminum cyminum)*. Cumin is a small species with bipinnate, ferny leaves and small white flowers in umbels; its seeds resemble those of the Fennel and are pleasantly aromatic. The mature spicy seeds are used to prepare the essence found in liqueurs (Kümmel, for instance) or in wines. Infusions of Cumin can, supposedly, cure colic and they have a diuretic, carminative and digestive action.

The fruits of the Common juniper *(Juniperus communis)* are known for their utilization in the kitchen as seasoning for sauces and other foods; in medicine they have a soothing, diaphoretic and diuretic action and can be used to cure bronchitis and cystitis. In external applications they are used for rheumatism and muscular pains.

To return to the subject of cooking, let us now mention some berries of alpine plants which are really excellent to eat. Amongst these we find the familiar bramble or blackberries, raspberries, bilberries such as the Whortleberry *(Vaccinium myrtillus)* which is rich in vitamin A, the Cranberry *(Vaccinium vitis-idaea)*, the small hairy berries of the Gooseberry *(Ribes grossularia)*, and the long, bunched, bright red, acid berries of the Barberry *(Berberis vulgaris)* which is used to make preserves. Perhaps we should also mention here that the bark and the roots of the Barberry contain an alkaloid which has a stimulating action on the vasomotor and respiratory centres of the body.

We find the most noble aromas among alpine plants in the wormwoods *(Artemisia* species*)* and the milfoils *(Achillea* species*)*. One of the most widespread species is the Common wormwood *(Artemisia absinthium)* which grows in the mountains and is also found at lower altitudes in arid, stony places. The flowering heads and the leaves are gathered and much used in the characteristic flavouring of vermouth and several liqueurs. In medicine it is used as a stimulant to the digestive system and to bowel movement; it was used frequently in the past as an agent to disperse worms and fever. Its abuse, however, can lead to terrible, chronic convulsions which are manifested in the disease known as 'absinthism'.

While on the subject of bitters and tonics we must of course mention the many species of gentian such as *Gentiana punctata, G. purpurea, G. acaulis, G. cruciata, G. verna, G. germanica, G. bavarica,* and above all, the Great yellow gentian *(Gentiana lutea)* whose large woody rhizomes are used in the manufacture of infusions and tinctures. Such preparations have a digestive and eupeptic action as well as being a heart stimulant. Care must be taken, however, when collecting the Great yellow gentian, not to confuse it with the poisonous Veratrum *(Veratrum album)*. In summer the Veratrum is easily recognized by its green-white flowers and it is, therefore, advisable to collect the rhizomes when the plant is in full bloom.

An expectorant and cough mixture can be

(Below left) Corydalis solida

(Below) Christmas rose (Helleborus niger) *in flower; this is a very poisonous plant*

made from the golden flowers of the very common mulleins *(Verbascum thapsus* and *V. phlomoides)* which can be gathered throughout the mountains from the lowlands right up to the alpine pastures. Recognition of these plants is quite straightforward; the yellow flowers are grouped into tall spikes which rise from rosettes of large, hairy leaves.

A sedative action, associated with anti-catarrhal properties and useful for diarrhoeic enteritis, can be obtained from a boiled preparation of the so-called Iceland moss which is actually a lichen, *Cetraria islandica,* common in the high pastures and the snow-filled valleys.

Mountain conifers are well known for the beneficial action of a few of the substances which can be derived from them in the treatment of coughs and bronchitis, and even as an auxiliary in the treatment of pulmonary tuberculosis. The active components of the various montane conifers include the turpentines and resins found in the Scots pine *(Pinus silvestris),* the White fir

(Abies alba), the Red fir *(Picea abies),* the Larch *(Larix decidua)* and particularly in the Mountain pine *(Pinus mugo* var. *mugo)* which is very rich in these products.

Among the most popularly used sedatives and refreshing drinks are those made from the Camomile *(Matricaria recucita),* a common lowland weed which is also often found at higher altitudes, and from various pansies such as the Hairy violet *(Viola hirta)* found in woodlands and the brilliant Long-spurred pansy *(Viola calcarata)* found on the alpine pastures.

The sweetish rhizomes of the Polypody *(Polypodium vulgare),* which is to be found frequently on the rocks and in the woods, act as laxatives. The Savin *(Juniperus sabina)* acts as a stimulant of the gastro-enteric mucous membranes and as an emetic; beyond small amounts, however, its use can be dangerous. The flowers and seeds of the Lily-of-the-valley *(Convallaria majalis)* have been known since biblical times for their properties as heart stimulants, diuretics and tonics.

Infusions of Silver birch leaves make useful bitters, with a diuretic and fever-alleviating action. Anti-diarrhoeic wines can be prepared by the addition of powder from the dried rhizomes of the Snakeweed *(Polygonum bistorta)*. In cases of muscular paralysis, alkaloids contained in the tubers of *Corydalis bulbosa* and *C. solida* have a sedative action.

In a book of this nature it would, of course, take too long to give a complete list of all the plant species which have medicinal properties. In many ways this is desirable since it is not advisable to advertise the full range of properties possessed by plants. The choice should be left to herbalists who are authorized to collect the plants and who also have the responsibility of establishing both the doses to be administered and the methods of administration of these medicines derived from our floral heritage. It must always be remembered that many montane and alpine plants which can be usefully employed for particular cures become harmful or actually poisonous if utilized indiscriminately.

It is, therefore, perhaps advisable to point out some of the more common poisonous species to be found in the mountains. The Savin *(Juniperus sabina)* can, as we have mentioned, cause serious damage of the kidneys if used excessively. We have also mentioned before that the Veratrum *(Veratrum album)* is often confused with the Great yellow gentian and possesses a rhizome which has a sour, bitter taste and is a very convulsive, irritant poison. The Mistletoe *(Viscum album)* is a parasite on pine trees and other conifers in the Alps and has the medicinal action of lowering blood-pressure, but it is also extremely poisonous and can damage the heart muscles. The Mountain anemone *(Pulsatilla montana)* with its dark blue or violet flowers is, like nearly all the *Ranunculaceae*, poisonous; it can cause violent, paralysing attacks of Bright's disease, while at the same time, if used carefully, is capable of curing neuralgia and other ailments. The Glacier buttercup *(Ranunculus glacialis)* is diaphoretic. Plants which have an irritant, convulsive effect include the Marsh marigold *(Caltha palustris)* the Globe flower *(Trollius europaeus)* and the Alpine clematis *(Clematis alpina)*. The Christmas rose *(Helleborus niger)* is a poisonous emetic which causes severe burns to the skin, throat and stomach. If carefully used, however, it can help to cure heart diseases. Other poisonous plants include the monkshoods *(Aconitum* species) and the columbines *(Aquilegia* species).

Everyone is aware of the danger of eating species of the *Umbelliferae* related to the Hemlock *(Conium maculatum)*, such as *Aethusa cynapium* and *Cicuta virosa*, but few know the danger in the common Tansy *(Tanacetum vulgare)* sometimes mistakenly collected for the liquor trade instead of its rarer variety *crispum*.

In the same way, few know of the highly vesicant action which a tincture of flowers of the Arnica *(Arnica montana)* can have on the skin of hyper-sensitive individuals. On the other hand, in many cases it is a very fine cure, if the patient can bear it, for outbreaks of boils and other skin diseases. Taken orally, in small doses, it can cure some coronary deficiencies and bronchial asthma.

So we must learn to recognize, during our mountain excursions, not only the loveliest flowers, but also the most useful and the most harmful ones. It must be remembered, however, that their use should always be directed by experts as if they were any other medicinal product.

Moreover, it is better to avoid indiscriminate gathering of aromatic and medicinal herbs. The collecting of such plants must be made according to very precise rules regulating not only the selection of the species, but also their phase of development, such as flowering and so on. We must avoid destroying the few wildernesses that remain nowadays, since so many plant species are being recklessly decimated by man.

A columbine, Aquilegia atrata; *most species of this genus are poisonous*

Alpine gardens

The beauty, value and rarity of the greater part of alpine plants, especially those with brilliantly coloured flowers, have always aroused the enthusiasm of floriculturists and nurserymen who wish to grow them either for study or to promote decorative species for commercial reasons. We should remember that alpine plants have slowly adapted to survive in their often difficult environment and so there is always the problem of growing these plants in places which are unsuitable for them, such as the lowlands. Attempts must be made either to alter the environment to suit the plants or to acclimatize the plants by studying the possibility of slow, gradual adaptations through the practice of hybridization. Such hybridization will produce more resistant species which can be successfully cultivated.

From the difficulties we have briefly stated it is obvious that the installation of an alpine garden in a mountain environment is a much better prospect than a garden of alpine flowers in the lowlands. In the latter case, however, a possible solution can be reached by means of a careful selection of those plants which can adapt to the new environment.

It is not only altitude which creates serious difficulties for the construction of the garden. Other important factors include the degree of exposure, the nature of the substratum, the amount of the water available, and the humidity.

There are many plants characteristic of acid soils and others characteristic of neutral or basic

View of the alpine woodland in the Munich Botanical Gardens showing a pond and a moss bed

soils, and this becomes all the more evident in the case of plants growing on debris, moraines and rocks which can either be siliceous (granite, gneiss and serpentine) or calcareous (limestone and dolomite).

And so the laying of an alpine garden involves a great deal of planning to give both environmental variety and a modest network of paths, steps and irrigation channels. Some of the things which should be included are hills with two slopes, valleys with varying exposure, rockeries, also with different aspects for both rock and steppe plants, little brooks and waterfalls, a marsh, a peat-bog, a pool with both gravelly and muddy banks, an arboretum, a nursery with sections that can be assembled for acclimatization and a small conservatory. Though many of these things may not be possible within the confines of a garden, it is obvious that the nearer they are approached the better.

Naturally the plan must be carried out without forgetting the aesthetic aspect of the layout.

(Top left) Alpine woodland (Munich Botanical Gardens).
(Top right) Pond and dwarf alpine plant bed (Cologne Botanical Gardens).
(Bottom left) Small pond surrounded by natural waterside plants (Garmisch, Bavaria)
(Bottom right) Rocks and shrubs (Munich Botanical Gardens)

View of a rocky sector in the 'Paridisia' alpine garden and of the Mountain Biology Station in the Gran Paradiso National Park, N. Italy

Chaotic jumbles, monotonous regularity or a counter-productive waste of space should all be avoided.

The economy of the garden requires the utilization, as much as is possible, of the material and the particular local structure of the soil. If there is a depression this can be exploited to produce water environments, and the rising ground, with suitable materials, can serve as the basis for the construction of mounds or rockeries.

In constructing rockeries it is necessary to provide the different structures found in nature. For instance, one needs large boulders with occasional crevices as well as compositions of smaller stones. Wide spaces between the rocks should be filled with earth that has similar chemical properties to those of the rock, in order to encourage the maximum growth of plants. A large 'ravine', will provide shelter for plants which like the shade such as *Viola biflora*, many saxifrages (such as *Saxifraga stellaris* and *S. rotundifolia*), members of the *Cariophyllaceae* and

(Left) A path in the 'Paridisia' alpine garden in the Gran Paradiso National Park, N. Italy

numerous ferns (such as *Cystopteris fragilis, Scolopendrium officinarum,* and *Asplenium adiantum-nigrum*).

We should remember that any area of soil left vacant will sooner or later, and often quite rapidly, be pioneered by plants of the surrounding flora. Regular invaders include weeds which infect uncultivated and arid land (for example *Poa annua, Polygonum aviculare, Myosotis arvensis, Taraxacum officinale, Trifolium repens* and some species of *Euphorbia*). In the heaps of earth and stones waiting to be cultivated one often finds the Rose bay willowherb *(Epilobium angustifolium)* and, near the heaps of manure, common weeds like the Good King Henry *(Chenopodium bonus-henricus)*, the Monk's rhubarb *(Rumex alpinus)* and Common nettles *(Urtica dioica* quickly spring up.

In these situations it is best not to collect up the weeds indiscriminately. Unless there is an urgent need for space some of the pioneering plants can be left to grow in the garden, and only those which have no decorative value or have become a pest need be uprooted.

A successful alpine garden requires, besides the various kinds of rocks we have already discussed, different kinds of soil; this is because each plant species needs its own particular type of substratum. For instance, there are ferns which need the acid type of soil found in chestnut woods, ericas which prefer iron-rich soil like that found in heaths, and some campanulas, globularias, and potentillas which like mineral-rich, reddish clays. It is therefore essential to have a supply of good meadow earth, forest soil, manure-rich loam, clay, fine sand, shingle, leaf litter, various types of peat, wall rubble and slaked lime.

(Right) Poppy plants in bloom; this species, Papaver nudicaule, *is extremely easy to cultivate*

To ensure that the garden is continuously in flower during both spring and summer, and to avoid too many blooms either in early spring or late autumn being crowded together the best method is to put together plants which have different characteristics. For instance, we can group together the Purple crocus *(Crocus purpureus)* and its relatives, the spring-flowering *Colchicum alpinum* and the Autumn crocus *(C. autumnale)*, along with the spring-flowering Wood anemone *(Anemone nemorosa)* and an autumn-flowering cyclamen, *Cyclamen europaeum.*

This process can obviously be extended and applied to all the common shrubs. The Sloe *(Prunus spinosa)* is a spring-flowering plant, together with its familial relative the Hawthorn *(Crataegus monogyna)*. These can be made into a hedge with the summer-flowering Dog rose *(Rosa canina)* and the autumn-fruiting Barberry *(Berberis vulgaris)* with its lovely scarlet berries.

The floral layout of a garden is always the most important problem to be solved. An alpine garden can be planned according to a systematic basis, following the groups dictated by plant classifications, or, alternatively, on ecological principles or even on a geographical basis. In the first case the plants must be grouped according to the family or the genus to which they belong. In this sense a rockery can be organized to provide environments for the stonecrops (of the genus *Sedum*), including, for example: *Sedum album, S. annum, S. rupestre, S. sexangulare, S. spurium, S. maximum, S. kamtchaticum* and *S. brevifolium.* All these colourful plants have slightly different ecological requirements.

Another rockery might be devoted to the houseleeks of the genus *Sempervivum* such as: *S. tectorum, S. montanum, S. arachnoideum, S.*

(Below) Example of a rock garden

(Right) Pyrenean poppy plant in full bloom (Mecanopsis pyrenaicum); this is one of the loveliest ornaments of rocky screes and is easily grown in alpine gardens

wulfenii, S. arenarium, S. magnificum and many others. Again attention must be paid to their particular preferences for types of soil.

Another good example for this type of rockery would be a collection of the very rich group of the saxifrages. Some of the most spectacular examples include: Saxifraga paniculata, S. cotyledon, S. lutea, S. rotundifolia, S. cuneifolia and S. longifolia. It must also be borne in mind that this genus, too, consists of many different ecotypes and it is obviously impossible to grow xerophytic species, which need little water, next to halophytic ones, which need continuous humidity. This situation leads to very complex problems in the distribution of the species around a relatively limited area with little environmental variation. Quite often this can be solved simply by separating the widely different plants with little partitions of stone, metal or plastic which become invisible as the plants develop.

The layout of a garden on an ecological basis, which is by far the most natural and modern method, groups the plants according to their characteristic environmental requirements.

Only in this way, for instance, can we attempt the far from easy task of creating a peat bed. It can be done, however, and once created provides a constant source of fascination, because in it we can assemble, in a few square metres, some of the interesting acid bog plants. These include the sundews, Drosera rotundifolia and D. longifolia, the butterworts like Pinguicula vulgaris, Primula farinosa, Dactylorchis maculata, Tofieldia calyculata, Parnassia palustris, and, among the shrubs, Empetrum nigrum, Vaccinium uliginosum or, if there is nothing better, the Ling or Common heather (Calluna vulgaris). The construction of a peat bed is made particularly difficult by the survival problems of the peatmosses of the genus Sphagnum. This problem arises mainly because it is essential that they have acidic water and far too often the correct pH of the soil is impossible to maintain.

One of the most interesting environments is the steppe-like habitat. This can be reproduced in a garden on one or more adjacent, rocky mounds. Here one could plant the Feather grass (Stipa pennata), Stipa capillata, Melica ciliata, Festuca ovina var. glauca, Carlina vulgaris, Echium vulgare, Achillea nobilis, Centaurea paniculata, Pulsatilla halleri, P. montana, Petrorhagia saxifraga, P. prolifera, some rare species of the genus Astragalus such as Astragalus centroalpinus, A. exscapus and A. uralensis, a few stonecrops (Sedum species), and, among the shrubs, the Common juniper (Juniperus communis) and its close relative, the Savin (Juniperus sabina).

Obviously, the contribution that exotic plants and artificially selected, cultivated species can make to the scene depends largely on the degree of purity and character that one considers desirable in order to make the setting a natural garden.

The third type of pattern which can be used for a garden layout is the geographical one. According to this pattern each sector of the garden is arranged so that plants which supposedly originated in the various continents, or in the mountain ranges that are part of them, are grown together. Obviously the difficulties of acclimatization arise once more. For instance, the cacti of the montane deserts of Arizona have very different ecological requirements from the famous Edelweiss of the Eurasian mountains. Thus, although this arrangement is botanically very interesting, it is extremely difficult to execute and needs a lot of resources.

Identification of alpine flowers

The remainder of this book is devoted to a series of brief descriptions of the most notable alpine flowers. These have been arranged, for ease of identification, in family or generic groups which are fairly well known. Botanical terms are explained in the glossary on page 127.

Anemones

Anemones are herbaceous, rhizomatous, perennial dicotyledons of the family *Ranunculaceae*. The leaves are either simple or variously deeply divided several times and frequently in verticills around the stems. The flowers vary in colour, but are generally white, yellow or violet; they are usually solitary but sometimes appear in clustered groups on the inflorescence. The sepals are free and petal-like, 5 or more in number, and the stamens are numerous. Most of the anemones belong to the three genera *Anemone*, *Pulsatilla* and *Hepatica*.

Pulsatilla alpina (Anemone alpina) White alpine anemone
Height 20–45 cm; perennial; the stem simple, rigid and hairy; the radical leaves with long petioles, hairy, triangular and bi- or tri-ternate pinnatisect; the stem leaves similar, but with short petioles; the flowers large with 6 or more petal-like sepals, white, backed with red; stamens numerous with yellow anthers. After flowering the individual carpels become a feathery, rounded mass.
Flowering June–August; found in alpine pastures.

Pulsatilla alpina **subsp.** *apiifolia (Anemone sulphurea)* Yellow alpine anemone
Similar to *P. alpina,* but with bright yellow flowers.

Pulsatilla vernalis (Anemone vernalis) Spring anemone
Height 2–15 cm; perennial, with a basal rosette of pinnate or ternate leaves divided into 2–3 segments; involucral sheath at the top of the flowering stem with purplish hairs which project beyond the flower; the flowers large and solitary, erect or frequently bent over with 6 (or more) petal-like sepals, pink-white inside, red-violet and hairy on the outside.
Flowering April–July; found in alpine pastures.

Pulsatilla halleri (Anemone halleri) Haller's anemone
This species is rather similar to the preceding one. Height 5–30 cm; perennial; the basal leaves hairy, bipinnatisect. The flowers with 6 red-lilac or purple petal-like sepals, which are at first bell-shaped, later becoming open and semi-erect.
Flowering April–July; found on screes.

Pulsatilla montana (Anemone montana, A. pulsatilla var. *montana)* Mountain anemone
Similar to *P. halleri* but smaller, with both the basal and the stem leaves more deeply divided and the entire plant villous; its flowers with 5–6 sepals, dark purple or clear violet in colour, bell-shaped at first and then open, though more pendulous. Perennial.
Flowering March–May; found in fields, pastures and open woods.

(Right) Larch and fir wood in the Aosta Valley; in the clearings of these woods and in their thick undergrowth it is always possible to find many magnificent alpine flowers

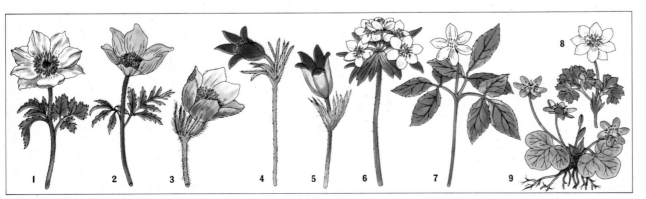

Comparative diagram of the principal species of anemones:
1 Pulsatilla alpina
2 P. alpina *subsp.* apiifolia
3 P. vernalis
4 P. montana
5 P. halleri
6 Anemone narcissiflora
7 A. trifolia
8 A. baldensis
9 Hepatica nobilis

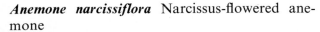

Anemone narcissiflora Narcissus-flowered anemone

Height 10–40 cm; hairy; perennial; the basal leaves long-petiolate, palmately lobed, with trifid or lance-shaped segments; the leaves of the involucre forming a tuft below the flowers, similarly deeply cut, but narrower and not petiolate; the flowers numerous, pedunculate, organized into umbels at the apex; the 6 petal-like sepals white, pink on the outside and hairy; the stamens numerous, with yellow anthers.

Flowering June–August; found in fields, meadows and cliffs.

Anemone ranunculoides Yellow wood anemone

Height 10–30 cm; perennial; the basal leaves palmately lobed with 3–5 dentate segments, each on a long petiole; the apical leaves form an involucre below the flowers; the flowers apical, yellow with 5–8 petal-like sepals (reminiscent of a buttercup flower).

Flowering March–June; found on mountains, fields and woods but uncommon.

Anemone nemorosa Wood anemone

Rhizomatous plant 10–20 cm high; perennial; basal leaves similar to those of the previous species, but the leaves of the involucre rather more deeply divided; the flowers with 6–12 oblong-elliptic, petal-like sepals, white or frequently flushed with pink or violet on the outside; stamens numerous with white anthers.

Flowering March–June; found in woods and glades.

Anemone trifolia

Rhizomatous perennial plant 10–30 cm high; leaves with 3 dentate segments; the flowers with 5–9 petal-like sepals, white or violet-red in colour.

Flowering March–July; found in fields and among rocks

Anemone baldensis Monte Baldo anemone
Perennial plant with a slender rhizome, 3–12 cm high, hairy; the lower leaves numerous, twice ternate, with dentate segments; the radical and involucral leaves sub-sessile; the flowers solitary, with long peduncles and 5–9 white, pink-backed sepals.
Flowering July–August; found in alpine pastures, cliffs and screes.

Hepatica nobilis (*H. trifolia, H. triloba, Anemone hepatica*) Hepatica
A caespitose plant 5–20 cm high; perennial, with basal leaves only. The leaves deeply divided, leathery, with 3 heart-shaped lobes, at first green, later becoming bright purple. The flowers long pedunculate, with 6–10 petal-like sepals, blue-purple, violet-lilac or rarely white in colour; beneath the flower the involucre consists of 3 leaves with the appearance of true sepals. The stamens

numerous with grey anthers.
Flowering February–May; found in woods and rough, stony places.

Pinks and Carnations

These annual or perennial herbaceous plants of the family *Caryophyllaceae* (dicotyledons) are characterized by lanceolate, often very narrow opposite leaves which are inserted on the stems at widely spaced and swollen nodes. The flowers consist of 5 deltoid petals with triangular to rhomboid limbs which are toothed or laciniate and have a tubular calyx and an epicalyx below. There are 10 stamens and 2 styles.

Dianthus carthusianorum Carthusian pink
Height 5–50 cm; perennial; stems rigid with distant inter-nodes; the leaves long and narrow, attenuate at the apex; flowers, usually one or more,

(Below) Narcissus-flowered anemone (Anemone narcissiflora)

(Top right) Hepatica (Hepatica nobilis)

(Bottom right) Wood anemone (Anemone nemorosa)

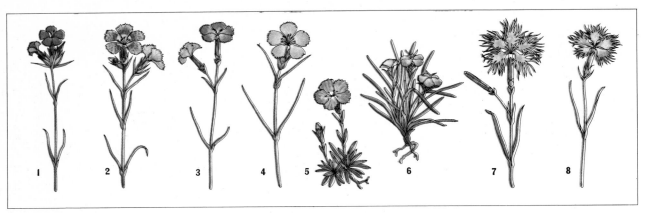

apical, red or purple in colour. The variety *atrorubens* has smaller flowers, with a much less intense colour.

Flowering May–August; found in open woods and stony pastures.

Dianthus seguieri Seguier's pink

Height 20–60 cm; perennial; the leaves linear-lanceolate; flowers relatively large and fragrant, pink or purple in colour, whitish below with a ring of dark spots at the centre; the petal limb long-dentate at the margin; the flowers in apical fasicles or rarely solitary.

Flowering June–October; found in stony places of the submontane zone.

D. inodorus is similar, but the flowers are paler, they lack a scent, and they are more generally solitary.

Dianthus silvestris Wood pink

Height 10–15 cm; perennial, with a spreading habit to form dense clumps; the basal leaves rather narrow and long; the stem leaves becoming smaller towards the top of the stem; flowers pink in colour, solitary or sometimes grouped into panicles, petal-limb toothed at the margin; the calyx tube very long cylindrical and with an epicalyx consisting of 2–4 scales.

Flowering July–August; found in woods, rocks and walls.

Dianthus pavanus (D. neglectus) Neglected or Mountain pink

Height 3–10 cm; perennial; stems usually in clumps but sometimes solitary; the leaves narrow, grass-like, rigid and pointed; the flowers generally solitary, brilliant rose-purple in colour; petals dentate.

Flowering July–September; found in grassy pastures and high alpine stony places, but it is very rare.

Dianthus alpinus

Height 3–20 cm; perennial; both rosette and stem leaves present, broad-oblong to lanceolate; the flowers solitary or in groups of 2–4, pink or purple in colour with patches of white.

Flowering June–September; found in alpine pastures and on calcareous rocks.

Dianthus glacialis

Height 3–10 cm; perennial; tufted; leaves narrow, slightly fleshy, sometimes extending beyond the flowers from grooved nodes; flowers solitary, pink in colour, white at the throat.

Flowering July–August; found in high alpine stony fields and on granite rock.

Dianthus superbus Superb pink

Height 20–90 cm or more; perennial; branching at the top to form sparse glaucous tufts; the leaves linear-lanceolate, pointed and coarse at the edges; flowers large, strongly scented, solitary or in groups of 2–5 on lateral peduncles, pink or purple (rarely white) in colour, with a yellow, hairy throat; petals deeply laciniate at the margins.

(Below) The small, common Carthusian pink (Dianthus carthusianorum)

Flowering April–September; found in stony fields.

Dianthus monspessulanus Fringed, or Montpellier pink

Height 5–60 cm; perennial; stems slender and undulating; the leaves linear and pointed; flowers fragrant, solitary or in groups of 2–7, white or pink in colour and occasionally bearded or fringed.

Flowering May–August; found in scrubby fields and rocky woods.

D. plumarius (Common pink) differs principally in being glaucous and having larger leaves.

Gentians

The gentians are, without doubt, among the most admired of the alpine plants because of their colour. They can be placed in two groups according to the flower colour, the first with blue or white flowers, and the second with red, yellow or purple flowers. They belong to the family *Gentianaceae* and are characterized by opposite leaves which are entire and without stipules, flowers with a distinct calyx of 4–5 sepals and a tubular corolla with 4–5 apical lobes. The illustration below shows many of the species described on the pages which follow.

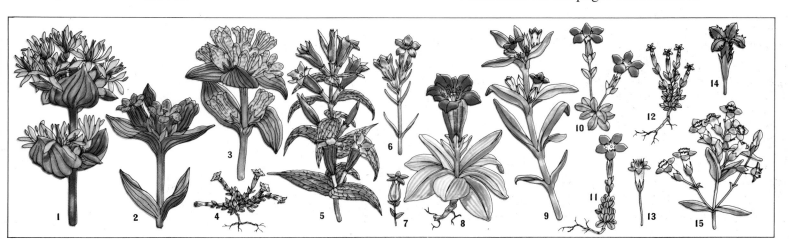

Gentiana lutea Great yellow gentian

Height 50–120 cm; perennial; erect, with a large woody rhizome, spreading roots and a rigid stem; leaves large, elliptical, acute, bright green in colour, with 3–5 veins on the lower surface and a fine network of reticulate veins on the upper surface; the flowers with a finely toothed calyx; the corolla yellow or rarely brick-red, rounded, with 5 deeply divided lobes.

Flowering June–August; found in alpine pastures.

Gentiana purpurea Purple gentian

Height 20–60 cm; perennial, erect plant with a woody rhizome; calyx as in *G. lutea;* the corolla bell-shaped, with petal-like lobes, purple, with dark spots on the inside, yellowish at the base.

Flowering June–July; found in alpine pastures.

Gentiana punctata Spotted gentian

As *G. purpurea* but with a yellowish corolla, violet spots and oblong, petal-like lobes.

Perennial; flowering June–July; found in alpine pastures.

Gentiana asclepiadea Willow gentian

Height of stem 15–100 cm; perennial; the roots slender and spreading; the leaves opposite and lanceolate, with an undulate margin, tapering at the apex; the flowers deep blue with lighter bands, reddish spots within and greenish at the base, generally in pairs forming long, leafy racemes; corolla lobes 5, acuminate.

Flowering July–August; found in mountain woods.

Gentiana pneumonanthe Marsh gentian

Height 10–40 cm; perennial; stem simple or rarely racemose above; the leaves widely spaced, linear-lanceolate, the lower ones diminutive; the flowers blue with 5 greenish lines, alternate or opposite.

Flowering July–September; found in damp, grassy places on mountain sides.

Gentiana acaulis *(G. vulgaris, G. kochiana)* Stemless gentian

Height 1–12 cm; perennial; the basal leaves in a rosette, lanceolate or elliptical, acuminate at the apex; the flowers solitary, large and usually dark blue (rarely violet, red or white), tubular inflated, with 5 pointed lobes; the calyx consists of 5 teeth, acuminate at the apex, with sometimes a small, inconspicuous membrane between the lobes.

Flowering May–August; found in chalky fields and pastures.

Gentiana clusii Trumpet gentian

As *G. acaulis* except for the elliptical, obtuse leaves and the well developed membrane between the teeth of the calyx.

Perennial; flowering May–August; found in acid fields and pastures.

Gentiana cruciata Cross gentian

Height 10–40 cm; perennial, with long roots; leaves in a basal rosette, lanceolate, obtuse, scabrid at the margin, the stem leaves crowded with narrow internodes; flowers numerous, in leafy racemes, azure-blue inside, greenish outside; the corolla tubular-campanulate with 4 petal-like lobes; calyx with 4 triangular teeth.

Flowering July–September; found in pastures and woods of the subalpine zone.

Gentiana verna Spring gentian

Height 2–20 cm; perennial; stem angled; the leaves in the basal rosette, ovate-oblong in outline; the stem leaves, generally in pairs, few or sometimes absent; the flowers with a finely toothed calyx; the corolla tubular, brilliant blue (or rarely white) in colour with 5 petal-like bifid lobes.

Flowering May–August; found in alpine pastures and rocky, grassy places.

Gentiana brachyphylla (*G. orbicularis, G. favratii*) Round-leaved gentian

Similar to *G. verna* but with obtuse or semi-orbicular leaves, the margins sometimes rough; the corolla dark blue inside, greenish outside, with obtuse lobes.

Perennial; flowering August–September; found in exposed and dry places.

Gentiana bavarica Bavarian gentian

Similar to *G. verna* but height 4–20 cm, with rounded cylindrical stems bearing 3–4 pairs of leaves; the leaves rounded at the apex; the calyx often violet and the corolla lobes deep blue (rarely white or violet), the base paler blue with obtuse, petal-like lobes.

Perennial; flowering July–September; found in damp alpine pastures.

Gentiana utriculosa Bladder gentian

Height 6–35 cm; annual; stem erect, branching; the leaves ovate-oblong, obtuse, with rough margins, those of the rosette being larger; flowers solitary or rarely branched; the calyx teeth lanceolate-acuminate, forming a wide tube with wings; the corolla small, intense blue in colour with 5 ovate lobes.

Flowering May–July; found in alpine pastures.

Gentiana nivalis Snow gentian

Height 2–30 cm; annual; the stem erect, branching from the base or rarely simple; the basal leaves, small and obovate, form a rosette; stem leaves lanceolate; the flowers small, intense dark blue in colour, with an angled, tubular calyx without wings; the corolla with 4–5 lobes only 3–4 mm long.

Flowering June–August; found in damp and boggy alpine pastures, stony places and scree-slopes.

Stemless gentian (Gentiana acaulis)

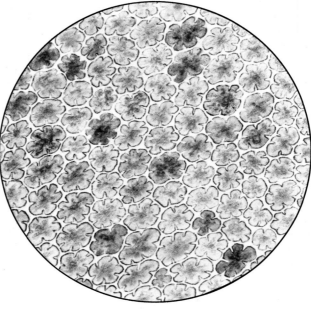

Stained tangential section of a flower of the Spring gentian (Gentiana verna)

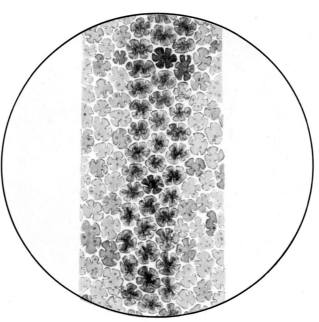

Transverse section of a flower of the Stemless gentian (Gentiana acaulis) *under the microscope; the greenish cells are those which give a metallic reflection to the flower*

(Above) Fringed gentian (Gentianella ciliata)

(Above right) Flowering plant of the Felwort (Gentianella amarella)

Gentianella ciliata *(Gentiana ciliata)* Fringed gentian
Height 5–30 cm; perennial, with one or more erect, angular stems; leaves not in a basal rosette, but in opposite pairs, lanceolate, rough at the margins; the flowers clear blue, with a long calyx having deeply laciniate, lanceolate teeth; corolla, with 4 long petals, fringed with hairs at the margin.
Flowering July–November; found in dry stony meadows and grassy woods.

Gentianella campestris *(Gentiana campestris)* Field gentian
Height 3–35 cm; annual or biennial; stems branching, angular; leaves oblong or lanceolate, the basal ones in a rosette; flowers numerous, blue-lilac (rarely white); the calyx with 4 irregular teeth; corolla with 4 petal-like lobes and with a fringed scale at the base.
Flowering July–October; found in fields and pastures.

Gentianella germanica *(Gentiana germanica)* Large field gentian
Similar to *G. campestris* but generally branching above and with longer internodes; the calyx angular and the corolla with 5 lobes, reddish-violet or violet in colour.
Usually biennial; flowering May–October; found in meadows on calcareous rocks.

Gentianella amarella Felwort
Height 2–30 cm; annual or biennial; similar to the 2 preceding species, simple, or branched only at the base; the leaves of the basal rosette lanceolate, narrow; those of the stem similar but longer; flowers red-violet (rarely white or yellow) with a 4–5 lobed calyx and corolla.
Flowering May–October; found in fields, pastures and heaths.

Primroses

Herbaceous plants, belonging to the family *Primulaceae* (dicotyledons). They are always perennial and have a basal rosette of leaves. The flowers are either single or in umbellate clusters. The calyx is 5-lobed, forming a tube, and the corolla is gamopetalous (petals united) with 5 petal-like, rounded lobes.

Primula vulgaris Primrose
Height 5–20 cm, with a basal rosette of oblong-ovate or obovate leaves narrowed at the base; the peduncles short, umbellate and the flowers sulphur-yellow or clear yellow in colour.
Flowering March–May; found in woods and banks on mountains.

Primula veris *(P. officinalis)* Cowslip
Height 10–30 cm; the leaves oblong-ovate and narrowed or heart-shaped at the base, irregularly toothed at the margin and hairy on the upper surface; the inflorescence in the form of an umbel of many scented flowers on short velvety peduncles; the calyx rather translucent, velvety and swollen above; the corolla with small lobes, golden yellow in colour.
Flowering March–June; found in woods and grassy places.

Primula elatior Oxlip, Paigle
Similar to *P. veris* but with more rugose leaves; the calyx not expanded towards the apex and less velvety; the corolla much larger and sulphur-yellow in colour.
Flowering March–August; found in open grassy woods and sheltered banks.

Primula auricula Auricula, Bear's-ear
Height 1–15 cm; the rosette leaves large, obovate, fleshy, narrowed to the petiole, often with a small toothed margin and the upper surface frequently

farinose; the inflorescence robust, with usually numerous, yellow, sometimes scented flowers with white farinose throats.

Flowering April–July; found on grassy crags and calcareous cliffs.

Primula farinosa Bird's-eye primrose

Height 3–20 cm; basal rosette of oblong or lancolate leaves, narrowed at the base, toothed, and usually farinose underneath; the inflorescence is generally many-flowered, the flowers small, pink with a yellow throat (in rare cases white or purple); the petal lobes consistently emarginate.

Flowering May–August; found in damp pastures and fields.

Primula hirsuta (P. viscosa) Red alpine primrose

Plant 1–7 cm high, with a more or less well-developed rhizome; leaves in various forms, from ovate to lanceolate in outline, sticky and irregularly toothed; inflorescence with an umbel of up to 15 flowers, pink, purple or, in rare cases, white, with a pale coloured throat; the petal-lobes emarginate.

Flowering April–August; found in pastures among rubble and on damp, siliceous rocks, crags and screes.

Primula allionii Allioni's primrose

An almost stemless plant with a long rhizome; the leaves oblong or rounded, greyish in colour, fleshy and sticky, with short petioles; inflorescence extremely short, bearing 1–7 pink or red-purple flowers.

Flowering March–May; found on crags and calcareous rocks.

Primula glutinosa Sticky primrose

Similar to *P. allionii* but the inflorescence 3–8 cm high with 2–8 scented flowers; the petals deep violet, viscid and deeply incised; the leaves sticky, oblong to lanceolate in outline.

Flowering June–August; found in pastures on granitic soils.

Primula marginata

Plant with a woody rhizome up to 20 cm long; leaves oblong or ovate, deeply toothed; young leaves and at least the edges of old leaves white-yellow and mealy; inflorescence 3–9 cm high with an umbel of 2–15 flowers; the flowers red-purple, lilac-violet or violet-blue; the petal lobes emarginate.

Flowering May–August; found on calcareous cliffs and scree slopes.

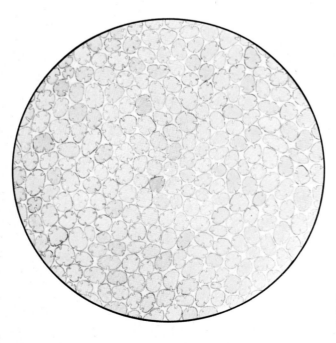

(Above left) Cowslip (Primula veris)

(Above) Bird's eye primrose (Primula farinosa)

Stained tangential section of a flower of the Bird's eye primrose (Primula farinosa)

(Right) Fine specimen of a Bear's ear (Primula auricula)

118

Primula minima Least primrose

A very small plant with a basal rosette of wedge-shaped or triangular leaves, with small teeth on the upper surfaces; the inflorescence up to 4 cm high with 1–2 sub-sessile flowers; the flowers pink with large, very deeply divided V-shaped petal-lobes.

Flowering June–July; found in grassy places and cliffs, especially in high mountains.

Buttercups

These plants are usually herbaceous perennials of the family *Ranunculaceae* (dicotyledons) and for the most part have deeply incised, palmate leaves. The flowers are either solitary or in many-flowered inflorescences, and are yellow, white or pink in colour, with 3–5 sepals and a similar or larger number of honey-leaves; there are numerous stamens and many united carpels within the corolla. Some of the species described below are cosmopolitan and not exclusively alpine.

Ranunculus aquatilis Common water crowfoot

A submerged aquatic plant with free floating stems; the leaves small, and of two types; those floating with a wide, lobed lamina with dentate margins, and those submerged deeply incised and filiform; the flowers white, with 5 petals.

Flowering March–September; found in slow flowing water.

Ranunculus pyrenaeus Pyrenean buttercup

Height 5–15 cm; the radical leaves lanceolate or linear, gradually narrowed at both ends, sessile; the stem leaves few, sessile; inflorescence with 1–4 white flowers, with 5–8 honey-leaves.

Flowering May–July; found in alpine pastures, especially when damp and calcareous.

Ranunculus parnassifolius

Height 5–20 cm; the basal leaves long petiolate, ovate-cordate and entire; the stem leaves narrow and sessile; the stems with corymbs of 1–20 white, pale pink or reddish flowers with rounded honey-leaves.

Flowering June–August; found in rocky places, especially on limestone and schist in high alpine areas.

Ranunculus alpestris Alpine buttercup

Height 3–12 cm; basal leaves petiolate with 3–5 deeply incised, overlapping, crenate, rounded lobes, palmate in outline; the stem leaves tri-

(Far left) Globe flower (Trollius europaeus)

(Left) Marsh marigold (Caltha palustris)

partite, simple or reduced to bracts; inflorescence with 2–3 flowers; sepals glabrous; petals 5 or more, cordate, with shallow notched apex.
Flowering June–September; found in damp alpine rocky fields, snow patches and pastures.

Ranunculus glacialis Glacier buttercup or crowfoot
Height 4–25 cm; the leaves fleshy, palmate, once or twice ternate and deeply divided; the flowers white or pink and sometimes purple, honey-leaves 5, entire with an emarginate apex.
Flowering July–September; found in damp, stony pastures, by alpine lakes and acid moors.

Ranunculus aconitifolius White buttercup
Height 20–50 cm; leaves palmate-divided, with 3–7 ovate or lanceolate segments; radical leaves with long petioles but the stem leaves (at least the uppermost ones) sessile; the flowers white, in apical cymes; the sepals pinkish, caducous; corolla with 4–5 honey-leaves; the stamens short.
Flowering May–August; found in grassy fields and woods.

Ranunculus ficaria Lesser calendine, Pilewort
Plant 5–30 cm high; glabrous, with club-shaped tubers; leaves basal, fleshy, ovate to heart-shaped with angular lobes, dark green, often with purple blotches towards the centre of the lobe; flowers yellow, solitary, with 8–12 oblong honey-leaves.
Flowering January–May; found in woods, damp banks, ditches and streams.

Ranunculus thora Thora buttercup
Height 5–30 cm; poisonous; radical leaves few or absent; the stem leaves large, sessile, round to kidney-shaped, truncate or heart-shaped at the base, upper edge toothed; flowers yellow, with 5 honey-leaves.
Flowering May–July; found in woods and steep pastures, on limestone.

Ranunculus repens Creeping buttercup
Plant 15–60 cm high, with branching stolons, rooting at the nodes; the leaves glabrous or hairy, palmate, split into 3 lobes and each lobe usually secondarily divided into 3 further lobes; the flowers golden yellow, large, with 5 honey-leaves; sepals hairy.
Flowering March–July; found in wet fields, damp banks and ditches, and by ponds.

Ranunculus acris Meadow buttercup
A species similar to *R. repens*, though taller and more slender; the leaves larger and shiny, palmate or 5-sided, divided into 3–7 segments; the flowers usually smaller.
Flowering April–October; found in fields from lowlands to subalpine habitats.

Ranunculus bulbosus Bulbous buttercup
A species similar to the preceding one but with the stem swollen at the base; the leaves smaller and generally hairy, often white-speckled, with 3 lobes, the segments wedge-shaped and toothed; the flowers yellow with 5 honey-leaves; sepals reflexed to the base.
Flowering April–July; found in meadows, banks, dry fields and wooded sunlit crags.

Ranunculus montanus (*R. geraniifolius*) Mountain buttercup
Plant 5–50 cm high; rhizomatous, more or less hairy throughout; lower leaves polygonal in outline, divided into 3 ovate or wedge-shaped segments, the central one trifid, the lateral ones bifid; upper stem leaves lanceolate; the flowers yellow, with 5 honey-leaves. This species is the type of a confused and variable group containing *R. oreophilus, R. carinthiacus, R. aduncus, R. grenieranus* and *R. govanii*.
Flowering May–August; found in pastures and on grassy slopes.

Comparative diagram of principal species of the buttercups:
1 Ranunculus aquatilis
2 R. parnassifolius
3 R. pyrenaeus
4 Callianthemum coriandrifolium
5 R. alpestris
6 R. ficaria
7 R. glacialis
8 R. thora
9 R. aconitifolius
10 R. repens
11 R. montanus
12 R. pygmaeus
13 R. acris
14 Trollius europaeus
15 Caltha palustris

Ranunculus pygmaeus

A small, slender species 2–8 cm high; leaves small, kidney-shaped, the basal ones bluntly trifid to pentafid, petiolate, the upper leaves few, 3–5 lobed and sessile; the flowers yellow, small, with semi-reflexed sepals.

Flowering July–August; found in high alpine zones, at the snow line, and in snow-covered valleys with scattered vegetation.

Trollius europaeus Globe flower

Height 10–100 cm, with erect stem; both basal and stem leaves petiolate, palmate and with 3–5 lobes, each lobe divided into 2–3 lanceolate segments, serrate; the flowers golden yellow, large with 5–15 pale, petal-like sepals and 5 or more spathulate honey-leaves. Poisonous.

Flowering May–July; found in damp fields, pastures and woods.

Caltha palustris Marsh marigold, Kingcup

Plant 5–60 cm high; caespitose, with creeping rhizomes; stems stout, hollow, and much branched; the leaves large, fleshy, glabrous, rounded, crenate, and petiolate or sessile; the flowers large, bright or golden yellow, with 5–10 petal-like sepals and honey-leaves lacking; the stamens numerous with golden yellow anthers.

Flowering March–August; found in damp fields and pastures, by ponds and streams.

Callianthemum coriandrifolium (Ranunculus rutaefolium)

Height 5–20 cm; the basal leaves long, petiolate, triangular, bipinnate or biternate, with rounded, slightly fleshy segments; the stem leaves similar but sessile; flowers white with 5–15 ovate honey-leaves, each with a golden spot at its base.

Flowering June–August; found on cliffs and zones of sparse vegetation near the snow line; rare.

Saxifrages

Herbaceous dicotyledons, belonging to the *Saxifragaceae* family. Mainly perennial, sometimes woody at the base, and generally with a basal rosette of leaves. The flowers are small, with 5 petals, grouped in cymes or panicles.

Saxifraga cotyledon Pyramidal saxifrage

Height 15–70 cm; perennial; the basal leaves in a dense rosette, lanceolate or spathulate in outline, up to 6 cm in length, glaucous, purple at the base, stiff, finely toothed and encrusted with lime; the inflorescence large, branching from the base, forming a rough pyramidal panicle; the flowers numerous, white, often spotted with red.

Flowering June–August; found in crevices in damp or dripping siliceous rocks.

Saxifraga paniculata (S. aizoon) Livelong saxifrage

A very variable perennial plant, 5–50 cm high; basal rosette of densely packed glaucous, ovate leaves, finely toothed at the margin and encrusted with lime; the inflorescence erect and rigid, branching in the upper part; the flowers white or pale cream, sometimes covered with red spots.

Flowering May–September; found on rocks, moraines and crags.

Saxifraga cuneifolia Wedge-leaved saxifrage

A stoloniferous plant 5–25 cm high; perennial; the basal rosette of orbicular-spathulate leaves, dark green above, violet-purple below, fleshy and toothed at the margin; the inflorescence small, erect, terminal, with minute white flowers.

Flowering June–August; found on shady, cool rocks, especially among mosses in coniferous woods.

Saxifraga rotundifolia Round-leaved saxifrage

A perennial, rhizomatous species 10–40 cm high; the leaves delicate, small, in a basal rosette, kidney shaped or orbicular, toothed at the margin and petiolate; the inflorescence slender, branching at the apex, with small star-like white flowers.

Flowering June–September; found in shady, damp or saturated places.

Saxifraga stellaris Starry saxifrage

Height 4–20 cm; perennial; stem horizontal; the basal leaves long, ovate or oblong, narrowed at the base and toothed at the apex; the inflorescence loosely branched, with small leaf-like bracts at the nodes; the flowers small, white and star-shaped.

Flowering June–August; found at edge of streams, bogs and dripping banks, usually on acid soils.

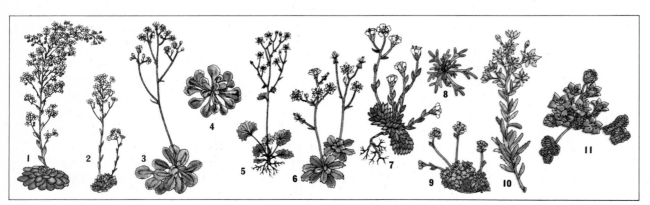

Comparative diagram of principal species of saxifrages:
1 Saxifraga cotyledon
2 S. paniculata
3 S. umbrosa
4 *Leaf rosette of* S. cuneifolia
5 S. rotundifolia
6 S. stellaris
7 S. muscoides
8 *Leaf rosette of* S. exarata
9 S. moschata
10 S. aizoides
11 S. oppositifolia

Saxifraga muscoides

Perennial plant forming a dense cushion of short, erect, tightly-packed shoots; leaves lanceolate with a 3-lobed apex; the flowering stems 5 cm or less, each with white or pale yellow flowers.

Flowering June–August; found on high alpine rocks and screes.

Saxifraga exarata Furrowed saxifrage

A variable, cushion-forming species with numerous short, hairy, branching shoots and small, narrow leaves, apically divided into 3–5 teeth; the inflorescence up to 10 cm high with 1–7 small, white, yellow or purple flowers, with obtuse, ovate to oblong petals.

Flowering and habitat as *S. muscoides*

Saxifraga aizoides Yellow mountain saxifrage

Sprawling, caespitose perennial up to 25 cm high, with slender leafy, hairy shoots; the leaves fleshy, oblong, hairy and sessile with a few marginal teeth; the inflorescence in a leafy cyme; the flowers star-shaped, yellow or orange in colour, in rare cases red, but sometimes red-spotted; some shoots sterile, and usually shorter than the flowering shoots.

Flowering June–September; found on shingle, damp, stony places and stream banks.

Saxifraga oppositifolia Purple saxifrage

A sprawling perennial plant combining several horizontal stems with numerous slender, branched upright ones in a loose mat or cushion; leaves green or glaucous, ovate-oblong, concave on the upper surface and sometimes ciliate, opposite and imbricate; the flowers solitary, pink-purple (in rare cases white), small, with elliptical petals; anthers violet-blue. A polymorphic species with at least 4 subspecies, often regarded as distinct.

Flowering June–August; found on moraines and in cracks in basic rocks.

Violets

Herbaceous dicotyledons belonging to the family *Violaceae*, with small, stipulate leaves; the basal ones are rounded, heart-shaped or even oblong, and are toothed or divided. The flowers are normally solitary (there are seldom 2) and are borne on long peduncles; they are spurred, variable in size and white, yellow, purple, blue or violet in colour. The flowers consist of 5 sepals and 5 free petals and are zygomorphic, that is they are symmetrical in the vertical plane only, having 2 upper pairs of petals and 1 lower, central spurred petal. There are 5 stamens alternating with, and concealed by, the petals.

Viola canina (Heath dog violet)
Herbaceous, arosulate, perennial, 5–40 cm high, glabrous, with woody creeping rhizomes; leaves heart-shaped or triangular, dentate, with lanceolate stipules; the flowers pale violet or rarely white, inodorous; the spur long, white or yellowish.
Flowering February–July; found in a wide range of habitats including moors, rocks, grass and woods.

Viola rupestris (V. arenaria)
A perennial species similar to *V. canina* but very much smaller; usually growing in clumps with a long creeping rhizome, terminating in a leaf rosette; the leaves heart-shaped or more or less rounded, and sometimes hairy; flowers with a long spur.
Flowering March–July; found in calcareous pastures and other open, fertile sites.

Viola mirabilis
A perennial, rosette-forming species, 5–10 cm high (after flowering may reach 20–30 cm), with a short rhizome; leaves ovate to heart-shaped or kidney-shaped, with an undulate margin; the stipules leaf-like, but hairy and with entire margins; the flowers initially arising from a rosette (later, smaller forms from ascending stems) large, usually sweetly fragrant, blue or pale violet in colour, with large spurs.
Flowering April–June; found in woodlands, on chalky soil; rather rare.

Viola hirta Hairy violet
A downy perennial, 5–15 cm high, with a short, thick, non-creeping rhizome, and lacking true stems; the leaf lobes large, ovate to heart-shaped or almost round, glaucous or hairy, with a toothed margin and hairy petioles; the stipules ovate to lanceolate, fringed with hairs; the flowers sweetly scented, or not at all, blue-violet in colour, or rarely white or white streaked with pink and violet.
Flowering March–June; found in woods.

The woods of tall conifers create environments which often hide very interesting plants

(Top) Comparative
diagram of principal
species of violets:
1 Viola canina
2 V. rupestris
3 V. mirabilis
4 V. hirta
5 V. pinnata
6 V. collina
7 V. cenisia
8 V. calcarata
9 V. tricolor

(Far left) Long-spurred
pansy (Viola calcarata)

(Left) Heath dog violet
(Viola canina)

Viola pinnata Finger-leaved violet

Perennial plant, 4–12 cm high, with a short, non-creeping rhizome; leaves arising from the top of the stock, fan-shaped, deeply dissected into equal lobes, ciliate; the stipules lanceolate, ciliate; the flowers small, odourless, pale violet or violet-blue, with a curved, blunt spur.

Flowering June–August; found on screes, rocks and calcareous alpine grassland; rare.

Viola biflora Yellow wood violet

A perennial plant 5–20 cm high; the leaves heart-shaped, rounded or kidney-shaped, with undulate margins, the lower ones long, petiolate; the stipules small, ovate to lanceolate, entire; the flowers small, yellow, with purple-brown lines, arising from slender, fragile peduncles.

Flowering May–August; found in damp places.

Viola cenisia Mt. Cenis pansy

Plant 3–5 cm high; perennial, with a branched rhizome; leaves small, the lower ones broadly ovate to round and the upper ones larger, oblong-ovate; stipules short, leaf-like or linear, on the upper leaves only; the flowers large, odourless, deep violet or lilac in colour.

Flowering June–August; found on calcareous screes and rocks, in high alpine areas.

Viola calcarata Long-spurred pansy, Mountain violet

Height 5–12 cm; perennial, with stems prostrate and slender; the leaves oblong; petiolate, entire or toothed; stipules entire or multi-divided; the flowers large, honey-smelling, lilac, blue, violet or yellow in colour with a long spur.

Flowering April–September; found in meadows, screes and pastures, usually above 1,500 m.

Viola bertolonii Bertoloni's violet

A perennial species similar to *V. calcarata* but with leaves of 2 types; the lower ones being small, ovate and toothed, with divided stipules, and the upper ones long, narrowly lanceolate; the flowers smaller and only violet or yellow in colour.

Flowering July–August; found in woods.

Viola tricolor Wild pansy, Heartsease

A slender annual, biennial or perennial, 3–50 cm high, with angular, simple to much branched stems; leaves of two types, the upper ones long and toothed, the lower ones rounded or oblong; the stipules divided; the flowers small, multi-coloured, blue-violet, deep yellow, white or pink, or combinations of these, and odourless.

Flowering March–September; found in cultivated ground and wasteland.

Glossary of botanical terms

Acuminate Becoming gradually pointed (as in a leaf).

Anther The stamen part containing pollen grains.

Apex/Apical The top (of a stem, leaf, etc.).

Arosulate Without a rosette.

Bi- (prefix) Two, or twice.

Bract Leaf-like appendages subtending a flower.

Caducous Falling off at an early stage.

Calcareous Basic soils containing free calcium carbonate.

Caespitose Dwarf (often rounded) tuft.

Calyx The sepals as a whole.

Campanulate Bell-shaped.

Carpel Floral part of the plant containing the ovaries.

Ciliate With regularly arranged hairs projecting from the margin.

Cordate Heart-shaped.

Corolla The petals as a whole.

Corona 'Crown' or top of a head.

Corymb Raceme with pedicels becoming shorter near the top so that the flowers are on the same level.

Crenate Regular rounded teeth.

Cyme An inflorescence whose growing points are each terminated with a flower, so that continued growth depends on the production of new lateral flowers.

Dentate Tooth-like.

Dicotyledon Those flowering plants with a pair of first leaves or cotyledons at germination.

Emarginate With a shallow notch at the apex.

Entire Not toothed or cut; complete (of leaves).

Epicalyx Calyx-like structure outside, but close to, the true calyx.

Farinose Mealy-textured like damp flour.

Fascicle Bundle.

-fid (suffix) Lobe-like projection.

Glabrous Without hairs.

Glaucous Blueish/greyish (often describing waxy covering).

Honey-leaves Petal-like parts of the flower with nectarines.

Inflorescence Flowering branch; portion of stem, bracts and flowers above the last stem leaves.

Imbricate Overlapping.

Internode Part of the stem between two adjacent nodes.

Involucre Bracts forming calyx-like structure around a condensed inflorescence.

Laciniate Deeply divided into narrow, irregular segments.

Lanceolate Spear-head shape (of leaves).

Linear Narrow, parallel-sided (of leaves).

Lobe Divided portion, but not separate leaflets (of leaves).

Node Point on the stem where one or more leaves arise.

Ob- (prefix) Inverted; an obovate leaf is broadest above the middle, an ovate leaf is broadest below the middle.

Obtuse Blunt.

Opposite Of two organs arising at the same level on opposite sides of the stem.

Orbicular Rounded, with length and breadth about the same.

Ovate Oval with pointed ends.

Palmate Consisting of more than three leaflets arising from the same point (of leaves).

Panicle Branched raceme.

Pedicel Stalk of a single flower.

Peduncle (pedunculate) Stalk of an inflorescence.

Petal The free lobe of a corolla in the flower; usually the coloured inner series.

Petiole Stalk of a leaf.

Pinnate Leaf composed of more than three leaflets arranged in two regular rows along a common stalk or rhachis.

Pinnatisect Regular division of the leaf into lobes, cut almost down to the midrib.

Polymorphic Of many forms (i.e. varieties, species, etc.).

Prostrate Lying closely along the surface of the ground.

Raceme/Racemose An unbranched inflorescence in which the flowers are borne on pedicels, usually conical in outline.

Radical   Arising from base of stem or rhizome.
Reflexed   Turned back upon itself.
Reticulate   Marked with a network of veins.
Rhizome   Underground stem lasting for more than one season.
Rosette   Circular group of leaves arising from a basal node (of leaves).
Rugose   Wrinkled.
Scabrid/Scabrous   Rough to the touch.
Scale   Membranous appendage.
Sepal   A member of the outer series of flower parts (calyx); usually green.
Sessile   Without a stalk.
Spathulate   Paddle- or spoon-shaped.
Spur   Hollow, narrow conical projection from the base of a petal or sepal.
Stamen   One of the male reproductive organs.

Stipule   Scale-like or leaf-like appendage at base of the petiole and sometimes joined to it.
Stolon (stoloniferous) Creeping overground stem of short duration, often rooting at the nodes.
Sub- (prefix)   Not quite, nearly.
Ternate   Divided into three equal parts (of leaves).
Tri- (prefix)   Three; i.e. trifid (split into three lobes).
Tuber (tuberous)   Swollen portion of root or stem of one year's duration; storage organ.
Tubular   Parallel-sided cylinder.
Umbel (umbellate)   An inflorescence in which the pedicels all arise from the same point at the top of a stem.
Undulate   Wavy in a plane at right angles to the surface.

Selected reading list

Barneby, T. P. *European Alpine Flowers in Colour*, Thomas Nelson, London 1967, 1968.

Clapham, A. R., Tutin, T. G. and Warburg, E. F. *Flora of the British Isles*, Cambridge University Press, Cambridge 1952, 2nd edn. 1962.

Corner, E. J. H. *The Life of Plants*, Weidenfeld & Nicolson, London 1964; New American Library, New York and Toronto 1968; New English Library, London 1968.

Eyre, S. R. *Vegetation and Soils: a World Picture*, Edward Arnold, London 1963; Aldine, Chicago 1963, 2nd edn. 1968.

Haviland, M. D. *Forest, Steppe and Tundra (Studies in Animal Environment)*, Cambridge University Press, Cambridge 1926.

Huxley, Anthony *Mountain Flowers in Colour*, Blandford, London 1967; Macmillan, New York 1968.

Odum, E. P. and H. T. *Fundamentals of Ecology*, W. B. Saunders, Philadelphia and London 1953, 2nd edn. 1959.

Oparin, A. I. *The Origin of Life* (translated from the Russian), Macmillan, New York 1938; 2nd edn. Dover Publications, New York 1953.

Peattie, R. *Mountain Geography (a Critique and Field Study)*, Harvard University Press, Cambridge, Mass. 1936.

Polunin, Nicholas *Introduction to Plant Geography and some Related Sciences*, Longmans, London 1960; Barnes & Noble, New York 1967.

Polunin, O. *Flowers of Europe: a Field Guide*, Oxford University Press, Oxford 1969.

Tutin, T. G. (Ed) *et al. Flora Europaea*, Cambridge University Press, Cambridge 1964–1972 (three volumes).

Acknowledgments

Sources of photographs on the following pages:
M. Pedone: 1, 9, 15, 24, 27 bottom, 28 bottom, 31 left, 38 top, 45 top right, 52 bottom row, right, 56, 59 right, 65 centre right, 68, 100, 113 top left, 117.
S. Stefenelli: 2, 4 top, 17, 38 bottom, 43 left, 45 bottom, 51, 73, 101, 102, 103, 104.
L. L. Rue/Bruce Coleman: 3.
P2: 4 bottom, 7, 8 bottom right, 13 right, 20 left, 21 right, 22 right, 26 bottom left, 28 top left, 31 right, 32 left, 36 right, 45 top centre, 49 top left, 52 top row, centre, 55 right, 62 bottom right, 63, 65 centre right, 66 right, 67, 70 top left, 72 bottom, 78 bottom left and right, 92 left, 96 right, 97, 98 right, 105, 106, 118 top left.
C. Bevilacqua: 5, 6, 11, 12, 13 left, 16, 20 right, 21 left, 22 left, 25, 26 top and bottom right, 27 top, 28 top right, 29, 30, 33, 36 left, 37 top left, 39 top right, 42, 43 right, 44, 47, 48, 49 top right, bottom left and right, 52 top row, left and right; second row, left and right; third row, all photographs; bottom row, left and centre, 53, 54, 55 left, 57, 58, 59 top left and bottom, 60, 61, 62 top and bottom left, 65 top and bottom right, 66 left, 69, 70 centre and bottom left, 71 top left and right and bottom right, 72 top, 74, 75 bottom left, 77, 78 top left, 91, 96 left, 98 left, 109, 110, 111 top and bottom right, 112, 116, 118 right, 120, 123, 126 left.
S. Frattini: 8 left, 23, 37 bottom, 39 centre, 45 top left, 50, 52 second row, centre, 62 top right, 64 bottom three photographs, 71 centre and bottom left, 75 top and bottom right, 78 top right, 107, 111 left, 113 right, 119.
G. Caprotti: 18, 40, 65 left, 70 right, 114, 125.
R. Longo: 32 right.
T. Schneiders: 34–35.
Grant-Heilman/Marka: 39 bottom, 99.
M. Fantin: 79, 86, 88–90, 92 right, 95.
N. Cirani: 80, 84, 85, 87.
E. J. Ott/Bruce Coleman: 81.
J. R. Simon/Bruce Coleman: 82–83.
M. Bavestrelli: 126 right.
Drawings on pages 108, 112–113, 120–122 and 126 redrawn from originals by D. Barry and M. Grierson in *Mountain Flowers in Colour* by A. Huxley (see reading list above).

21 February 2000

21 February 2000